MONGOLIA

THROUGH

THE AGES

A CONCISE GUIDE

By

Martin Miller-Yianni

COPYRIGHT AND ACKNOWLEDGEMENTS

Publisher: M P Miller-Yianni, Bulgaria

First Printing Edition 2024

ISBN 978-619-7742-55-8 (paperback)
ISBN 978-619-7742-56-5 (ePub)

A CIP catalogue record for this book is available from:

The National Register of Published Books in Bulgaria
bulevard 'Vasil Levski' 88,
1504 Sofia,
Bulgaria

Cover Design:
By Fadhil Abhimantra from unsplash.com

Title Page Image:
Ulaanbaatar, Mongolia
By Alexander Popovkin from Unsplash.com

i

ABOUT THE BOOK

"Mongolia Through the Ages: A Concise Guide" offers an accurate reflection of Mongolia's exclusive history. As part of a series on the histories of various nations, the book is written with meticulous attention to detail and a firm commitment to accuracy. Yet even with academic rigour it remains accessible to readers of all levels.

One of the key strengths of this book is its comprehensive yet detailed exploration of Mongolia's past. Each section delves into the complexities of Mongolia's numerous historical eras, offering readers clear insights into the forces that have shaped the nation across the centuries. Given the intricate nature of Mongolia's past, there are many points where historical events overlap, and readers will notice instances where a restatement of events in one chapter is repeated in the next. This repetition is inevitable, as it allows for a thorough understanding of how key developments are interconnected across different periods. Rather than being a hindrance, this approach helps reinforce the reader's insight, solidifying their grasp of the historical narrative.

The author steers the transitions between historical eras, providing summaries with of crucial people, events and places. These not only maintain the continuity of Mongolia's historical tale but also helps readers contextualise the intricacies of its past.

Whether one wishes to deepen their understanding of specific historical periods or gain a broader comprehension of Mongolia's historical journey, this volume offers an abundance of reliable knowledge and astute analysis. Spanning the achievements and challenges of ancient nomadic empires to the cultural changes of recent times, each chapter draws readers into the story of Mongolia's development through to its present day.

Contents

The coat of arms of Mongolia, adopted on 25 March 1992, embodies the nation's rich history, cultural heritage, and future aspirations. At its centre is a circular shape, symbolising unity and the eternal cycle of life, with a vibrant blue background representing the "Tenger," the eternal sky, a significant element in Mongolian spirituality.

At the top sits the golden Garuda, or Khangarid, symbolising protection and power, reflecting Mongolia's Buddhist and ancient shamanistic traditions. The Dharmachakra, a Buddhist symbol of righteousness, is central to the design, representing spiritual truth. Inside it lies the Soyombo, a national icon featuring a flame for vitality, the sun and moon for eternity, and the yin-yang symbol for balance.

Beneath the Dharmachakra is Mount Sumeru, symbolising strength and stability, along with a lotus flower, representing purity and spiritual potential. The emblem is bordered by a golden frame featuring traditional Mongolian patterns, symbolising prosperity and good fortune.

This post-socialist design replaced the Soviet-era coat of arms, which focused on industrial and agrarian symbols. The modern coat of arms reintroduces traditional Buddhist and historical elements, reflecting Mongolia's independence, resilience, and forward-looking identity while honouring its heritage.

The flag of Mongolia, adopted on 12 February 1992, reflects the nation's history, culture, and identity, representing both its rich past and modern statehood. It consists of three vertical bands, with the outer red stripes symbolising strength, courage, and resilience, while the central blue stripe represents the eternal sky, "Tenger," central to Mongolian spirituality. The blue also symbolises peace, freedom, and Mongolia's vast natural landscape.

The Soyombo symbol, in gold on the left red stripe, is a key element. Designed by Zanabazar in the 17th century, it holds profound cultural meaning. At the top is a flame with three tongues, representing the past, present, and future, symbolising Mongolia's continuity. Below are the sun and moon, symbols of eternity, reflecting Mongolia's enduring existence and the natural cycles that govern life. Two downward-pointing triangles represent the strength and determination of the Mongolian people to defend their nation.

At the centre of the Soyombo is the yin-yang symbol, symbolising balance and harmony, while the two rectangles flanking it represent unity and stability. The bottom triangles reinforce the message of resilience and strength.

The current flag replaced the socialist-era version, which included a star representing communist ideology. Its redesign in the 1990s marked Mongolia's transition to a democratic republic, reflecting a return to traditional values while embracing a free and independent future. The flag symbolises the country's resilience, connection to nature, and commitment to sovereignty and unity.

Mongolia a landlocked country in East Asia, sits between two of the world's largest nations, Russia to the north and China to the south, east and west. Its geographic coordinates span from latitudes 41°35' to 52°09' N and longitudes 87°44' to 119°56' E. Despite no coastline, Mongolia's location is strategically significant, historically acting as a vital link between East Asia and Europe, particularly along the ancient Silk Road.

Covering an area of approximately 1.56 million square kilometres, Mongolia is the 18th largest country in the world. Its vast territory includes diverse landscapes, from the arid Gobi Desert in the south to the mountainous regions of the Altai and Khangai in the west and centre. The country's proximity to both Russia and China have influenced its geopolitical role, serving as a buffer state and a bridge for trade, culture, and diplomacy. Mongolia's central position in the Eurasian continent, combined with its sparse population, creates a unique blend of isolation and strategic importance in regional and global affairs.

CHAPTER 1

The Land and Its People

MONGOLIA'S LAND AND PEOPLE

Mongolia is a vast and enigmatic land, where centuries of history and culture are deeply intertwined with its rugged, often unforgiving environment. From the towering, snow-capped peaks of the Altai Mountains to the vast, arid expanse of the Gobi Desert, Mongolia's geography is as varied as it is extreme. Its landscapes, while harsh, have nurtured a way of life that has endured for millennia, shaping not only the physical character of the country but

1

also the spirit of its people. Central to this spirit is the nomadic lifestyle—a defining feature of Mongolian identity, which has withstood the challenges of time, political upheavals, and the encroachments of modernity.

GEOGRAPHY AND LANDSCAPE: AN OVERVIEW OF MONGOLIA'S UNIQUE ENVIRONMENT

Mongolia's geographic diversity plays an essential role in its cultural and historical development. Covering an area of approximately 1.56 million square kilometres, it is one of the largest landlocked nations in the world. However, despite its vastness, Mongolia is one of the least densely populated countries, home to a mere three million people, many of whom still live in close communion with nature. This low population density speaks to the challenging environments that dominate the country, demanding both resilience and adaptability from those who call it home.

To the south lies the iconic Gobi Desert, one of the largest and driest deserts in the world, stretching across the southern third of Mongolia into northern China. The Gobi is not a desert of endless sand dunes, as one might imagine, but a strikingly diverse landscape featuring bare rock, gravel plains, and sparse, hardy vegetation. Temperatures in this region are known for their dramatic fluctuations, ranging from scorching highs in the summer to freezing lows in the winter, forcing inhabitants and wildlife to adapt to the extremes of the environment. Despite its barren appearance, the Gobi has long been an important area for nomadic herders, who rely on its meagre yet sustainable grasslands to graze their livestock, particularly camels, goats, and sheep.

THE GOBI DESERT

In stark contrast, the Altai Mountains dominate the far west of Mongolia, a magnificent and rugged range that serves as both a natural barrier and a cultural boundary. These towering peaks, many reaching over 4,000 metres, are among the highest in Central Asia and are often snow-covered for much of the year. The mountains create a unique climate zone, providing rivers and lakes that sustain life in this otherwise harsh region. The Altai, with its alpine meadows, glacial valleys, and snow-fed rivers, offers a striking juxtaposition to the dry, desert regions further south. Here, yaks and horses thrive in the cooler, more temperate conditions, and the people who inhabit this area have developed distinct cultural practices, including eagle hunting, which has become emblematic of western Mongolian nomadic life.

Between these two extreme landscapes lies Mongolia's vast steppe, a sprawling expanse of grassland that has long been the heartland of the Mongolian people. The steppe, with its

3

seemingly endless horizons and rolling hills, is a landscape perfectly suited to the nomadic lifestyle. It is this region that has seen the rise of great empires, most notably that of Genghis Khan and the Mongol Empire, which once stretched across much of Eurasia. The steppe's rich pastures provide grazing grounds for livestock, particularly horses, which are central to Mongolian culture and history. The nomads of the steppe live in close harmony with their environment, moving with the seasons to ensure their animals can find the best grazing land and water sources.

Nomadic Life: A Resilient Cultural Identity

The nomadic lifestyle is the beating heart of Mongolia's cultural identity, a way of life that has endured for centuries despite the pressures of modernity. The essence of Mongolian nomadism lies in its adaptability and flexibility, shaped by the practical need to survive in an environment that is both beautiful and inhospitable. While the world around Mongolia has changed dramatically, the fundamentals of nomadic life have remained remarkably consistent, ensuring the survival of this ancient tradition.

Central to Mongolian nomadism is the concept of mobility. Unlike sedentary agricultural societies, Mongolian nomads are constantly on the move, following the cycles of nature. This movement is not random but guided by the knowledge of the land and the seasons, passed down through generations. In the summer, herders may move their families and livestock to higher altitudes, where cooler temperatures and fresh pastures are more conducive to the wellbeing of their animals. In winter, they return to more sheltered areas, often in valleys, where their herds can be protected from the worst of the cold. This seasonal migration, known as 'otor', is a well-calibrated system designed to maximise the health of livestock and ensure the sustainability of the environment.

The nomadic family structure plays a crucial role in the success of this lifestyle. Families live in 'gers'—the iconic circular, portable dwellings made of felt and wood—designed to be easily assembled and dismantled as the family moves from one grazing ground to another. The 'ger' is more than just a practical solution to mobility; it is a symbol of Mongolian life, embodying the values of simplicity, functionality, and harmony with nature. Inside the 'ger', life is centred around the hearth, where meals are prepared and warmth is provided during the long, harsh winters. The space within the 'ger' is carefully organised, with different areas designated for men and women, for work and rest, reflecting the structure of Mongolian family and society.

Livestock is central to the nomadic way of life, not only as a source of food, but also as a marker of wealth and social status. Horses, in particular, hold a revered place in Mongolian culture. Mongols are often said to be 'born in the saddle,' and horsemanship is a skill taught from an early age. Horses provide transport, milk, and meat, but they also carry a deep cultural significance, symbolising freedom, strength, and the indomitable spirit of the Mongolian people. The annual Naadam festival, with its horse racing, wrestling, and archery competitions, is a celebration of these skills and the endurance of nomadic traditions.

Despite the encroachment of modernisation and urbanisation, many Mongolians continue to maintain their nomadic lifestyle. In recent decades, economic changes and environmental challenges such as overgrazing and climate change have posed significant threats to the sustainability of nomadic practices. Yet, the resilience of this culture remains evident. Mongolian nomads have shown a remarkable ability to adapt, integrating modern technology into their lives in ways that do not fundamentally alter their relationship with the land. Solar panels, for example, are now a common sight in the countryside, providing energy for lighting and communication, while satellite phones and motorbikes coexist alongside traditional methods of transport and communication.

THE MONGOLIAN 'GER'

Mongolia's nomadic culture, therefore, stands as a testament to the enduring human capacity to live in harmony with nature. It is a way of life that, despite its challenges, continues to offer a profound connection to the land and a sense of identity that transcends the march of time. In a world that is increasingly globalised and disconnected from the natural environment, Mongolia's nomads serve as a reminder of the value of simplicity, resilience, and a deep-rooted respect for the land.

SUMMARY:

The previous chapter introduced Mongolia's dramatic landscapes, from its rolling steppes to its forbidding deserts and mountain ranges. This challenging environment cultivated a unique way of life, where nomadic herding and a deep bond with nature were essential to survival. Mongolian society evolved around this landscape, with traditions, social structures, and even spiritual beliefs intimately tied to the land. This chapter sets the stage for understanding how Mongolia's natural world shaped its people, creating a culture defined by adaptability, resilience, and a distinctively nomadic spirit.

DID YOU KNOW?

Mongolia's unique style of throat singing, known as 'khöömei', has ancient roots, blending music with nature. This technique allows singers to produce two or more pitches at once, imitating natural sounds such as flowing rivers and mountain winds, reflecting Mongolia's deep connection to its vast landscapes and spiritual heritage.

CHAPTER 2

Ancient Mongolia

C. 10,000 BCE – 3000 BCE

ANCIENT MONGOLIA

*O*ften romanticised as the land of horsemen and nomads, Mongolia boasts a rich and complex history that stretches back thousands of years. Before the rise of the Mongol Empire under Genghis Khan, this region was home to a succession of nomadic cultures and tribal confederations that played a significant role in shaping Central Asia's political and cultural *landscape. From the earliest prehistoric settlements to the formation of powerful tribal alliances, Mongolia's ancient history offers a window into the origins of the steppe peoples who would later come to dominate Eurasia.*

Prehistoric Settlements (10,000 BCE – 3,000 BCE)

The history of human habitation in Mongolia dates back to the Palaeolithic era, when early hunter-gatherer societies began to explore and settle in the region. Archaeological evidence from this period reveals the presence of nomadic communities who traversed the land in search of game and natural resources. These early inhabitants would have faced a challenging environment, with the Mongolian plateau being subject to extreme temperatures and varying climates. Nevertheless, the abundance of game, from mammoths to deer, made it a viable region for prehistoric humans.

The Orkhon Valley, one of Mongolia's most fertile and historically significant areas, has yielded some of the earliest evidence of human habitation. Archaeologists have discovered tools, weapons, and primitive structures that suggest a longstanding presence of humans in the region. These early settlers would have lived in small, mobile communities, moving frequently to follow the herds of animals that provided their sustenance. By around 10,000 BCE, humans had spread across much of Mongolia, gradually developing more sophisticated hunting techniques and tools as they adapted to their environment.

Migration patterns during this time likely followed the flow of rivers and the availability of water sources, particularly in the more arid regions of the Gobi. Some archaeological findings indicate seasonal movement between mountainous regions and lower plains, suggesting an early form of nomadism that would become a defining feature of Mongolian life in the millennia to come. By the late Neolithic period, around 3,000 BCE, Mongolian inhabitants had begun experimenting with rudimentary forms of agriculture, though the harsh climate of the region meant that pastoralism remained the dominant form of subsistence.

THE ORKHON VALLEY

THE BRONZE AGE AND EARLY STEPPE CULTURES (3,000 BCE – 300 BCE)

The Bronze Age marked a significant turning point in Mongolia's early history, as technological advancements and social organisation began to take shape. Between 3,000 BCE and 300 BCE, the nomadic cultures of the Mongolian steppes became more complex, with the emergence of distinct tribal identities and new forms of warfare. Bronze metallurgy spread throughout the region, revolutionising tool-making and weaponry, which, in turn, transformed the way early Mongolians lived, fought, and traded.

Among the early steppe cultures that rose during this time were the Xiongnu, a formidable confederation of nomadic tribes that emerged as one of the first major powers in Central Asia. Though often remembered for their later conflicts with China, the Xiongnu's origins can be traced to the early Bronze Age cultures that roamed the Mongolian steppes. Archaeological findings, including burial mounds and rock carvings, provide insights into the life of these early nomads, highlighting their expertise in horse-riding, archery, and metalwork.

The Xiongnu were not alone in shaping the steppe's early history. Other nomadic groups, often less well-known, left their mark on the region's development. These tribes, like their Xiongnu counterparts, relied heavily on pastoralism, moving their herds of horses, sheep, and cattle across the vast plains in search of seasonal pastures. The horse, in particular, became an increasingly central figure in these early steppe cultures. As nomads mastered horseback riding, they gained unprecedented mobility, which allowed them to cover great distances and engage in trade and warfare with neighbouring regions.

Trade with nearby civilisations, such as China, began to increase during this period. The Mongolian steppe, while isolated geographically, became a crossroads for the exchange of goods, ideas, and technology between East and West. Bronze weapons, tools, and jewellery found in Mongolian burial sites point to interactions with more sedentary societies, especially in regions to the south. The harsh, open landscape of Mongolia encouraged the development of mobile, militarised societies that could defend their resources and expand their influence across Central Asia.

A BRONZE AGE MONGOLIAN BELT BUCKLE, 2ND CENTURY BCE

RISE OF TRIBAL CONFEDERATIONS (300 BCE – 500 CE)

As the Bronze Age gave way to the Iron Age, the political and social landscape of Mongolia began to evolve dramatically. From around 300 BCE, powerful tribal confederations started to emerge, solidifying the Mongolian steppes as a major centre of nomadic culture and power. Among these early confederations, the Xiongnu, Xianbei, and Rouran played key roles in shaping the history of the region, each leaving an indelible legacy on Mongolia and the surrounding areas.

The Xiongnu Confederation, which had its roots in earlier steppe cultures, became the dominant force in Central Asia by the 3rd century BCE. The Xiongnu were an aggressive and highly organised nomadic empire, known for their ability to field large cavalry forces and conduct raids deep into Chinese territory. The Xiongnu are most famous for their prolonged conflict with the Han Dynasty of China, a series of wars that lasted for over a century and led to the construction of the Great Wall as a means of defending against Xiongnu incursions. At the height of their power, the Xiongnu controlled vast swathes of territory, including much of Mongolia, and engaged in both warfare and diplomacy with the great civilisations of the time.

Following the decline of the Xiongnu in the 1st century CE, another nomadic confederation, the Xianbei, rose to prominence. The Xianbei, though less centralised than the Xiongnu, played a significant role in the history of the Mongolian steppe. Their influence extended beyond Mongolia into northern China, and they are credited with establishing some of the earliest known steppe empires. Under the leadership of Tanshihuai, a Xianbei chieftain, the Xianbei confederation reached its peak in the 2nd century CE, controlling a vast territory and exerting influence over both the Chinese and the Central Asian nomads.

The Rouran, another major confederation, succeeded the Xianbei and continued the tradition of nomadic dominance in Mongolia. Active from the 4th to the 6th century CE, the Rouran are perhaps best known as the precursors to the Mongols, sharing many cultural and political traits with the later Mongol Empire. Like their predecessors, the Rouran relied on their formidable cavalry forces to project power across the steppes and into China. They established one of the earliest known steppe empires, which would serve as a model for future nomadic confederations. Their decline in the mid-6th century, following defeat at the hands of the Göktürks, marked the end of a significant era in Mongolia's early history.

These tribal confederations laid the groundwork for the later Mongol Empire by establishing patterns of nomadic governance, warfare, and social organisation that would be refined and expanded upon by Genghis Khan and his successors. While each of these early confederations eventually fell, their legacies lived on, contributing to the deep historical and cultural continuity of Mongolia's nomadic traditions.

THE DOMINATION OF THE ROURAN CONFEDERATION

SUMMARY:

As explored in the last chapter, ancient Mongolia was a land of tribes, each self-sufficient and skilled in survival on the harsh steppe. By around 10,000 BCE, these early communities had developed a robust culture centred on horse-riding, hunting, and pastoralism. Though disparate, the tribes shared a lifestyle of mobility and a reliance on the land, qualities that would later facilitate their remarkable unity under the Mongol Empire. This early era set down the roots of Mongolian identity, one based on independence, resourcefulness, and kinship, which later forged a pathway to regional dominance.

DID YOU KNOW?

In ancient Mongolian culture, horses were far more than transport or livestock; they held spiritual significance and were seen as companions for life and beyond. Some tribes believed the spirits of fallen warriors resided within the horses of the clan, a belief that infused their close bond with these animals with reverence and symbolism.

PEOPLE:

Prehistoric Hunter-Gatherers (c. 10,000 BCE – 3000 BCE) - These early inhabitants of Mongolia survived by hunting large animals like woolly mammoths and reindeer, as well as foraging and fishing. Although their names are unknown, they were vital in establishing human presence in the region, adapting to the harsh climate and developing the skills necessary for survival in the steppes.

Stone Tool Craftsmen (c. 5000 BCE – 3000 BCE) - This group of early people significantly advanced the crafting of stone tools, which were crucial for survival in Mongolia. Their ability to develop more efficient tools and weapons reflects the growing cognitive abilities of these ancient peoples, aiding in hunting and shaping their environment.

PLACES

Orkhon Valley (Evidence from c. 5000 BCE) - The Orkhon Valley in north-central Mongolia became a central location for human activity in ancient times. Archaeological evidence suggests that it was an early settlement area, and it later became a crucial region for nomadic cultures and empires, contributing to Mongolia's long history of human habitation.

Khovsgol Lake (Inhabited c. 8000 BCE – 3000 BCE) - Northern Mongolia's Khovsgol Lake, one of the oldest freshwater lakes in the world, was home to prehistoric peoples. The abundant resources of the lake and surrounding area made it an ideal settlement location, evidenced by the remains of tools and other artifacts found there.

Gobi Desert Region (Inhabited c. 10,000 BCE – 3000 BCE) - Early human activity in what is now the Gobi Desert shows that it was once a more habitable region. Stone tools and other archaeological evidence reveal that humans lived and thrived in the area before it became the arid desert it is today.

EVENTS

End of the Last Ice Age (c. 10,000 BCE) - The retreat of glaciers at the end of the Ice Age transformed Mongolia's landscape, making it more suitable for human habitation. This event coincided with the arrival of the first humans to the region, who benefited from the expanding flora and fauna.

Emergence of Neolithic Culture (c. 5000 BCE) - Around this time, Mongolia's prehistoric people began crafting polished stone tools, domesticating animals, and developing early agriculture. These changes marked a transition from purely nomadic lifestyles to more organised forms of society, paving the way for future cultural developments.

The Use of Pottery (c. 4000 BCE) - The introduction of pottery during this period indicates that Mongolia's early peoples were beginning to settle down and store food. Pottery remains found in the region suggest a shift towards more stable communities and complex societal organisation.

CHAPTER 3

The Mongol Empire

1162 – 1259

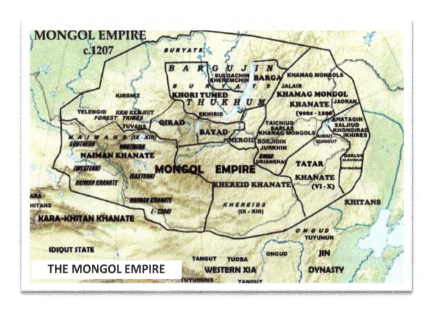

THE MONGOL EMPIRE

*T*he Mongol Empire, the largest contiguous empire in history, was born out of the vision, ambition, and military genius of one man: Genghis Khan. From the unification of warring Mongol tribes to the vast conquests that stretched across Eurasia, the story of the Mongol Empire is a testament to the power of leadership, strategy, and adaptability. Under Genghis Khan *and his successors, the Mongols forged an empire that reshaped the political, economic, and cultural landscape of the medieval world, laying the foundations for modern globalisation through their promotion of trade, communication, and stability across vast distances.*

TEMUJIN'S RISE (1162 – 1206)

The story of the Mongol Empire begins with the life of Temujin, the man who would become Genghis Khan. Born around 1162 near the Onon River in what is now northeastern Mongolia, Temujin's early life was one of hardship and struggle. His father, Yesügei, was a minor chieftain, but when he was poisoned by a rival clan, Temujin's family was cast out, and they were forced to live in poverty on the harsh Mongolian steppe. These early experiences of betrayal and survival in an unforgiving environment profoundly shaped Temujin's character, instilling in him a relentless drive for power and a deep understanding of the importance of loyalty and unity.

As a young man, Temujin faced numerous challenges, including captivity and the constant threat of attack by rival tribes. However, he quickly proved himself a charismatic leader and a brilliant tactician, gaining the loyalty of key allies through his ability to forge strategic marriages and alliances. One of the most important relationships in his early rise to power was his bond with Jamukha, a childhood friend and fellow warrior. Together, they initially fought side by side, but their relationship eventually soured, leading to a series of conflicts that would culminate in Temujin's rise as the undisputed leader of the Mongols.

ONON RIVER LOCATION IN NORTHEAST MONGOLIA, TEMUJIN'S BIRTHPLACE

The Mongolian steppe during Temujin's youth was a fragmented and violent region, dominated by tribal warfare and shifting alliances. Temujin's vision was to unite the Mongol tribes under a single banner, creating a powerful and cohesive force capable of defending against external threats and conquering new territories. He pursued this goal through a combination of diplomacy, warfare, and innovation. One of his key strategies was to break the traditional Mongolian tribal structure, which was based on family and kinship ties, and reorganise his forces into units based on loyalty to him rather than tribal allegiance. This allowed him to create a more flexible and disciplined army, ready to act on his commands.

A series of key battles against rival tribes and confederations solidified Temujin's power. His victory over the Merkits, a tribe that had kidnapped his wife Börte, demonstrated his ability to wage war effectively and exact revenge on his enemies. His eventual defeat of Jamukha and the powerful Naiman tribe in 1204 was a turning point, after which Temujin became the uncontested ruler of the Mongol steppes. In 1206, Temujin was proclaimed Genghis Khan, meaning "universal ruler," by a council of Mongol leaders, marking the formal unification of the Mongol tribes and the birth of the Mongol Empire.

GENGHIS KHAN AND HIS WIFE BÖRTE

THE GREAT MONGOL CONQUESTS (1206 – 1227)

With the Mongol tribes united under his leadership, Genghis Khan turned his attention outward, launching a series of military campaigns that would expand the Mongol Empire across Central Asia, Persia, and into Europe. The Mongol conquests were characterised by their speed, brutality, and strategic brilliance, as Genghis Khan and his generals employed innovative tactics and psychological warfare to overwhelm their enemies. Central to the success of the Mongol army was its mobility and discipline. Mongol warriors, highly skilled in horseback archery, could cover vast distances quickly, striking with precision and retreating before their enemies could organise a defence.

One of Genghis Khan's first major campaigns was against the Western Xia kingdom in northwestern China, which he attacked in 1209. The Western Xia, although formidable, were no match for the Mongols' superior tactics, and by 1210, they had submitted to Genghis Khan, paying tribute and becoming a vassal state. This victory opened the door to further campaigns in China and Central Asia, as Genghis Khan sought to eliminate potential threats to his burgeoning empire.

In 1211, Genghis Khan launched an invasion of the Jin Dynasty in northern China, a wealthy and powerful state that had long dominated the region. The Mongol army employed a combination of siege tactics, psychological warfare, and mobility to dismantle Jin defences. By 1215, the Mongols had captured the Jin capital, Zhongdu (modern-day Beijing), marking a decisive victory. However, Genghis Khan's ambitions extended far beyond China. His next major target was the Khwarezmian Empire, which controlled much of modern-day Iran, Turkmenistan, Uzbekistan, and Afghanistan.

The conflict with the Khwarezmian Empire began in 1219 after a diplomatic dispute escalated into full-scale war. The Mongols, enraged by the execution of a Mongol envoy by the Khwarezmian ruler, Shah Ala ad-Din Muhammad, launched one of their most devastating campaigns. The Mongol army swept through Khwarezmian territory with unmatched ferocity, sacking cities such as Bukhara, Samarkand, and Nishapur. The Mongols employed a scorched-earth policy, destroying agricultural lands and massacring populations, sending a clear message to their enemies: resistance was futile. By 1221, the Khwarezmian Empire had been utterly destroyed, and Genghis Khan's empire now stretched from the Pacific Ocean to the Caspian Sea.

Genghis Khan's conquests also extended into Europe, as his generals Subutai and Jebe led campaigns into the Caucasus and eastern Europe. In 1223, the Mongols defeated a combined force of Russian and Kipchak warriors at the Battle of the Kalka River, further demonstrating the Mongols' military prowess. Although Genghis Khan himself did not live to see the full extent of Mongol expansion into Europe, his campaigns laid the groundwork for future Mongol incursions into the region.

By the time of Genghis Khan's death in 1227, the Mongol Empire had become the largest land empire in history. His conquests not only reshaped the political map of Asia and Europe but also set the stage for a new era of trade, cultural exchange, and communication across Eurasia.

BATTLE OF THE KALKA RIVER IN 1223

THE PAX MONGOLICA (1227 – 1259)

After Genghis Khan's death, his empire was divided among his sons and grandsons, but despite this fragmentation, the Mongols continued to expand their territory and influence. The period from 1227 to 1259 is often referred to as the 'Pax Mongolica'—the "Mongol Peace"—a time of relative stability and prosperity across the Mongol-controlled regions of Eurasia. Under the leadership of Genghis Khan's successors, particularly his third son Ögedei and his grandson Kublai Khan, the Mongols fostered an environment in which trade, communication, and cultural exchange flourished.

One of the most significant aspects of the 'Pax Mongolica' was the stabilisation of the Silk Road, the ancient trade route that connected the East and West. The Mongols, with their highly mobile and disciplined armies, were able to secure and protect the vast network of trade routes that spanned their empire. This allowed merchants, travellers, and diplomats to move more freely and safely than ever before. Goods such as silk, spices, precious metals, and textiles flowed across Eurasia, linking China, Persia, the Middle East, and Europe in a vast, interconnected trade system. The Mongols also facilitated the exchange of ideas, technologies, and religious beliefs, contributing to the spread of knowledge and innovation.

The Mongol Empire's system of governance was key to maintaining order across its vast territories. While the Mongols were often ruthless in conquest, they were pragmatic rulers who allowed a great degree of local autonomy. They employed a meritocratic system, promoting capable individuals regardless of their ethnic or religious background. The Mongols were also tolerant of different religions, allowing Buddhists, Muslims, Christians, and others to practise their faiths freely within their empire. This religious tolerance helped to create a more harmonious and diverse society, attracting scholars, artisans, and merchants from all corners of the known world.

THE SILK ROAD THAT CONNECTED THE EAST AND WEST

Ögedei Khan, who succeeded Genghis Khan as Great Khan, oversaw the continued expansion of the empire into Europe and the Middle East. His reign marked the height of Mongol power, as Mongol armies pushed westward into Poland, Hungary, and the Balkans, defeating European forces at the Battle of Legnica and the Battle of Mohi in 1241. Ögedei also continued to strengthen the empire's infrastructure, building roads, postal stations, and administrative centres to better manage the vast territories under Mongol control.

After Ögedei's death in 1241, a period of internal strife ensued, as various factions within the Mongol ruling family vied for power. However, despite these struggles, the Mongol Empire remained a dominant force, and the 'Pax Mongolica' endured for several more decades, particularly under the rule of Kublai Khan, who would go on to establish the Yuan Dynasty in China.

The 'Pax Mongolica' not only facilitated the exchange of goods and ideas but also helped to create a new global consciousness, connecting distant regions and peoples in ways that had never been possible before. The legacy of this period is evident in the blending of cultures and technologies that took place across Eurasia, influencing the development of both the East and the West for centuries to come.

SUMMARY:

Following our exploration of Mongolia's ancient tribes, this chapter introduced the rise of Temujin, who would become Genghis Khan, uniting warring clans and transforming Mongolia into the core of a vast empire. Through sheer military brilliance and strategic foresight, the Mongol Empire extended its influence across Eurasia, reshaping entire societies from China to Europe. By the time of Genghis Khan's successors, the empire was at its zenith, a formidable network of trade and cultural exchange that would leave an enduring mark on world history.

DID YOU KNOW?

The Mongol Empire's sophisticated postal relay system, the Yam, stretched across Asia and Europe, facilitating communication within the vast empire. With relay stations and mounted couriers, messages could cross thousands of miles rapidly, laying the foundations for advanced communications networks in Eurasia.

PEOPLE

Genghis Khan (1162 – 1227) - Born as Temüjin, Genghis Khan united the Mongol tribes and founded the Mongol Empire in 1206, creating one of the largest empires in history. Through his brilliant military tactics and ability to organise, he conquered vast regions from China to Persia. Genghis Khan is remembered not only for his conquests but also for fostering trade, establishing legal codes, and promoting religious tolerance within his empire.

Ögedei Khan (1186 – 1241) - The third son of Genghis Khan, Ögedei succeeded his father as Great Khan in 1229. Under his rule, the Mongol Empire continued its expansion, conquering much of Eastern Europe and the Middle East. He also helped stabilise the empire by building cities and improving administrative structures. Ögedei's leadership extended the Mongol Empire to its largest geographical size.

Tolui (1192 – 1232) - Genghis Khan's youngest son, Tolui was a skilled general who played a crucial role in his father's military campaigns, particularly in China and Central Asia. Although he never became Great Khan, Tolui's descendants, including his sons Möngke and Kublai, went on to lead and further expand the Mongol Empire.

PLACES

Karakorum (Founded in 1220) - As the capital of the Mongol Empire under Genghis Khan, Karakorum became a political and cultural centre. Located in the Orkhon Valley, it housed important administrative and religious buildings. Although Karakorum was eventually abandoned, it symbolised the power of the Mongol Empire during its early years.

Khentii Mountains (Birthplace of Genghis Khan) - These mountains, located in northeastern Mongolia, are traditionally regarded as the birthplace of Genghis Khan. The area held spiritual significance for the Mongols and served as a strategic stronghold for the rise of Genghis Khan and his unification of the Mongol tribes.

Bukhara (Conquered in 1220) - Bukhara, a key city in Central Asia, was captured by Genghis Khan in 1220 during his campaign against the Khwarezmian Empire. Its fall marked a significant milestone in the Mongol conquest of Central Asia. Genghis Khan's conquest of Bukhara is often remembered for his famous speech addressing the city's citizens, declaring his divine mandate to rule.

EVENTS

Unification of the Mongol Tribes (1206) - In 1206, Genghis Khan united the fractured Mongol tribes under his rule, formally establishing the Mongol Empire. This event marked the beginning of Mongol expansion, as the newly united tribes launched a series of military campaigns that would eventually lead to the conquest of much of Asia and Europe.

Conquest of the Khwarezmian Empire (1219 – 1221) - Genghis Khan's campaign against the Khwarezmian Empire, prompted by the execution of his envoys, resulted in the complete destruction of the empire. The conquest, which included the fall of major cities like Samarkand and Bukhara, demonstrated the Mongols' devastating military power and established their dominance over Central Asia.

Möngke Khan's Reign (1251 – 1259) - Möngke, the fourth Great Khan, solidified Mongol control over China and launched campaigns into the Middle East. His reign was marked by the continuation of the empire's expansion and the establishment of stronger administrative systems. His death in 1259 led to a succession crisis that eventually contributed to the division of the Mongol Empire into different khanates.

CHAPTER 4

The Golden Horde and Successor Khanates

1227 - 1680

THE GOLDEN HORDE

*T*he fragmentation of the Mongol Empire into various successor states following the death of Genghis Khan led to the emergence of several powerful khanates that continued to exert Mongol influence across Asia, the Middle East, and Eastern Europe. Among these were the Golden Horde, the Ilkhanate, and the Chagatai Khanate, each playing significant roles in shaping *the political, cultural, and economic landscapes of their respective regions. These successor khanates represented the continuity of Mongol power and governance, though each adapted differently to the local circumstances they encountered, from the vast steppes of Central Asia to the heartlands of the Islamic world.*

DIVISION OF THE EMPIRE (1227 – 1260s)

Upon the death of Genghis Khan in 1227, the Mongol Empire, which stretched from the Pacific Ocean to Eastern Europe, entered a period of internal fragmentation. According to Mongol tradition, the empire was divided among his sons and grandsons, each inheriting a section of the vast territory. This division, while meant to preserve family unity, eventually led to the formation of distinct political entities that operated independently. Genghis Khan's eldest son, Jochi, had died before his father, but his descendants were awarded the westernmost part of the empire, which became known as the Golden Horde.

The descendants of Genghis Khan's son Tolui, notably his grandson Kublai Khan, would go on to rule the Yuan Dynasty in China, while other grandsons established the Ilkhanate in Persia and the Chagatai Khanate in Central Asia.

The split of the empire also coincided with growing political and military conflicts between the successors. The different khanates began to assert their autonomy and pursue their own regional agendas, often leading to rivalry and even warfare between them. This division marked the beginning of the end for the unified Mongol Empire, as it gradually transformed into a collection of successor states that, while maintaining some cultural and political links, functioned as independent powers.

THE GOLDEN HORDE (1240 – 1502)

The Golden Horde, established by Batu Khan, a grandson of Genghis Khan, was one of the most influential Mongol successor states. Initially part of the greater Mongol Empire, it became a dominant force in Russia and Eastern Europe following Batu Khan's campaigns, which culminated in the Mongol invasion of Kievan Rus' and the subsequent establishment of Mongol dominance over the principalities of the region.

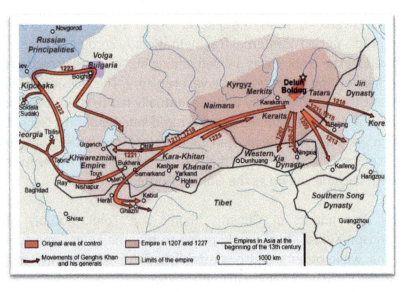

MAP OF THE EXPANSION OF THE MONGOLIAN KHANATES

At its height, the Golden Horde ruled over vast territories that extended from the Carpathian Mountains to the Siberian steppes and from the Ural Mountains to the Black Sea. Its political centre was located at Sarai, near the lower Volga River, from where it governed a network of vassal states, including many of the Russian principalities. The Horde imposed a system of tribute,

30

allowing local rulers to maintain some autonomy in exchange for regular payments and loyalty to the khans.

Despite its military strength, the Golden Horde eventually began to weaken due to internal strife, economic challenges, and the resurgence of Russian power. By the late 14th century, under the leadership of Tokhtamysh, the Golden Horde attempted to reassert its dominance, but it faced setbacks, including a devastating invasion by the Central Asian warlord Timur (Tamerlane) in 1395. Over the course of the 15th century, the Golden Horde fragmented into smaller khanates, including the Crimean Khanate, the Kazan Khanate, and the Astrakhan Khanate, marking the end of its unified control. In 1502, the final remnants of the Golden Horde were destroyed by the Crimean Khanate, which was aligned with the Ottoman Empire.

THE ILKHANATE AND THE MIDDLE EAST (1256 – 1353)

The Ilkhanate was founded by Hülegü Khan, another grandson of Genghis Khan, following his conquests in the Middle East. Hülegü led a series of brutal campaigns in the region, including the infamous sack of Baghdad in 1258, which marked the end of the Abbasid Caliphate and significantly altered the political and cultural landscape of the Islamic world. The Ilkhanate controlled much of modern-day Iran, Iraq, and parts of Turkey, Armenia, and Georgia, establishing its capital in Tabriz.

Initially, the Mongols of the Ilkhanate were religiously tolerant, practising a form of shamanism and Buddhism while allowing other faiths to coexist. However, under the reign of Ghazan Khan, who converted to Islam in 1295, the Ilkhanate became an Islamic state, adopting the Persian administrative system and culture. This shift helped integrate the Mongols into the predominantly Muslim societies they ruled, fostering a blending of Mongol and Islamic traditions. The Ilkhanate also played a crucial role in facilitating trade between East and West, acting as a bridge for the Silk Road.

Despite these achievements, the Ilkhanate began to decline in the early 14th century due to internal disputes over succession, economic difficulties, and external threats, particularly from the Mamluks of Egypt and the rising power of Timur. By the mid-14th century, the Ilkhanate had fragmented into several smaller states, losing its central authority. Its last ruler died in 1353, and the territory was absorbed into various regional powers.

THE CHAGATAI KHANATE AND CENTRAL ASIA (1227 – 1680)

The Chagatai Khanate, named after Chagatai Khan, the second son of Genghis Khan, governed the vast regions of Central Asia, including parts of modern-day Kazakhstan, Uzbekistan, Kyrgyzstan, and western China. While initially a unified state, the Chagatai Khanate eventually split into two regions: Western Chagatai (Transoxiana) and Eastern Chagatai (Moghulistan). The khanate played a key role in continuing Mongol influence in Central Asia, preserving Mongol traditions and culture long after the empire's fragmentation.

The Chagatai Khanate maintained strong ties to the Mongol way of life, especially the nomadic traditions of the steppe, and its rulers often vacillated between adopting sedentary governance and maintaining the more fluid, mobile society of their ancestors. The western part of the khanate, Transoxiana, became an important centre for Islamic scholarship and culture, while the eastern part remained more isolated and nomadic.

Over time, the Chagatai Khanate faced numerous challenges, including internal divisions, external threats from neighbouring states, and the rise of powerful Central Asian leaders such as Timur, who conquered much of the western Chagatai region in the late 14th century. Timur's conquests effectively diminished the power of the Chagatai rulers, though the eastern part of the khanate persisted until the late 17th century. By 1680, the Chagatai Khanate had largely ceased to exist as a coherent political entity, with its territory absorbed by the expanding powers of Russia and China.

CHAGATAI KHAN 'S STATUE IN MONGOL PALACE, GACHUURT MONGOLIA

As we delved into after examining the empire's peak, the Mongol Empire's fragmentation gave rise to powerful successor states such as the Golden Horde. These khanates, though geographically and politically distinct, upheld Mongol heritage across Asia and parts of Eastern Europe. They fostered an era of continued influence where Mongol customs, governance, and trade routes thrived, blending with local cultures and reshaping the regions they controlled. Each khanate developed its unique identity, yet all bore the legacy of the great Mongol Empire, maintaining its influence well beyond its fall.

DID YOU KNOW?

The Golden Horde maintained extensive trade with both Eastern and Western territories, and tea, introduced through these networks, became highly valued at the khan's court. Khan Öz Beg, for example, established tea as a diplomatic gift, highlighting its role in strengthening alliances and showcasing Mongol adaptability to foreign customs.

PEOPLE

Batu Khan (1207 – 1255) - A grandson of Genghis Khan and the founder of the Golden Horde, Batu Khan led the Mongol invasion of Eastern Europe, including the famous conquest of Kievan Rus' between 1237 and 1240. His leadership established the Golden Horde as a dominant Mongol power, controlling vast territories in Russia and Eastern Europe for over two centuries.

Berke Khan (1209 – 1266) - As the third ruler of the Golden Horde, Berke is notable for his conversion to Islam and his alliance with the Mamluks against his cousin Hulagu Khan's forces. Berke's reign marked a shift in the Golden Horde's policies, particularly his efforts to consolidate power and extend influence into the Islamic world.

Uzbek Khan (1282 – 1341) - Ruling the Golden Horde from 1313 to 1341, Uzbek Khan was instrumental in spreading Islam throughout the khanate. He is remembered for his religious policies and for stabilising the Golden Horde's economy, promoting trade with both Europe and the Islamic world during his long reign.

PLACES

Sarai (Founded c. 1240) - Sarai was the capital of the Golden Horde, founded by Batu Khan along the Volga River. It became a major political, economic, and cultural centre of the Mongol Empire in Europe. Sarai's strategic location allowed the Golden Horde to control trade routes between Europe and Asia and to manage vast territories.

Kazan (Founded c. 1400s) - Located along the Volga River, Kazan became one of the most important cities in the successor khanates, particularly the Kazan Khanate. It served as a key hub of commerce and a centre for Islamic culture after the fragmentation of the Golden Horde. The city's later conquest by Ivan the Terrible in 1552 marked the decline of Mongol power in the region.

Crimea (Conquered c. 1440s) - The Crimean Khanate, one of the successor states of the Golden Horde, played a vital role in the geopolitics of the Black Sea region. Its strategic location made it a centre for trade and a key ally of the Ottoman Empire, maintaining

Mongol influence in Eastern Europe until its annexation by Russia in 1783.

EVENTS

Mongol Invasion of Europe (1237 – 1242) - Led by Batu Khan, the Golden Horde's invasion of Eastern Europe devastated regions such as Kievan Rus', Poland, and Hungary. This series of campaigns marked the high point of Mongol expansion in Europe, establishing Mongol rule over vast territories and shaping the political landscape of Eastern Europe for centuries.

Conversion to Islam (1313) - Uzbek Khan's conversion to Islam and subsequent promotion of the religion throughout the Golden Horde had a lasting impact on the region. This event not only helped strengthen ties with the Islamic world but also altered the cultural and political identity of the Golden Horde, paving the way for the rise of Islamic successor khanates.

Fall of the Golden Horde (c. 1502) - The final collapse of the Golden Horde occurred when the Crimean Khanate, one of its successor states, defeated the remaining forces of the Horde. The once-mighty empire had already fractured into several smaller khanates, including the Kazan, Astrakhan, and Crimean Khanates, each of which continued to exist but with significantly reduced power and influence.

The Fall of Kazan (1552) - The Russian conquest of the Kazan Khanate by Ivan the Terrible marked a decisive moment in the decline of Mongol influence in the region. The fall of Kazan effectively ended Mongol rule over much of Russia and signalled the rise of the Russian Empire as a dominant power in Eastern Europe.

Decline of the Crimean Khanate (1680s) - Although the Crimean Khanate survived longer than other successor states, by the 1680s it had entered a period of decline due to internal strife and external pressures from Russia and the Ottoman Empire. Its weakening would eventually lead to its annexation by Russia in 1783, marking the end of Mongol-derived political influence in the region.

CHAPTER 5

Mongolia Under the Yuan Dynasty

1271– 1368

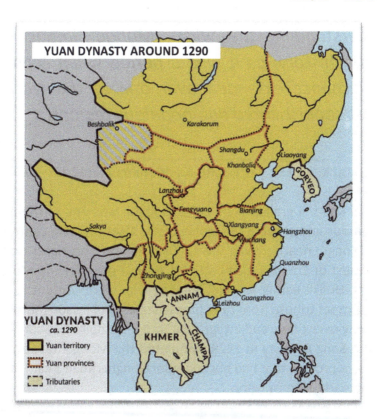

YUAN DYNASTY AROUND 1290

YUAN DYNASTY
ca. 1290

- Yuan territory
- Yuan provinces
- Tributaries

*T*he Yuan Dynasty, established by Kublai Khan, was a significant period in the history of both China and Mongolia. As the first non-Han

37

dynasty to rule all of China, the Yuan Dynasty marked the height of Mongol power and influence in East Asia. It was a time of cultural integration, economic growth, and administrative reform, though internal struggles and external pressures would eventually lead to its downfall. Mongolia's relationship with China during the Yuan Dynasty is crucial to understanding the wider Mongol impact on world history, as it was a period when Mongol governance extended over one of the world's most sophisticated and populous regions.

KUBLAI KHAN AND THE FOUNDING OF THE YUAN (1271 – 1294)

Kublai Khan, a grandson of Genghis Khan, was one of the most ambitious and capable Mongol leaders. After securing control of the Mongol heartlands in the 1260s, Kublai set his sights on the conquest of China, which had long been a prize for the Mongol rulers. Unlike earlier Mongol leaders, who were content to raid and extract tribute from the Chinese states, Kublai sought to rule directly over China and integrate it into his empire. His conquest of the Song Dynasty in 1279 completed the Mongol takeover of China, a process that had begun under Genghis Khan's campaigns in the early 13th century.

In 1271, Kublai Khan declared the founding of the Yuan Dynasty, formally claiming the Mandate of Heaven and presenting himself as the legitimate emperor of China. By adopting the dynastic title and incorporating Chinese Confucian traditions into his rule, Kublai sought to win the loyalty of his Chinese subjects while maintaining the traditional Mongol identity. His capital, Khanbaliq (modern-day Beijing), became the political and cultural centre of the Yuan Dynasty and the Mongol Empire.

Kublai Khan's rule was marked by a blend of Mongol and Chinese governance styles. While Mongol nobility and military leaders maintained significant influence over the administration, Kublai adopted Chinese bureaucratic practices to manage the vast population and territory of China. This included the use of the Confucian civil service system, though Mongols and other non-Chinese peoples were often given higher status within the government. Kublai also promoted trade, expanding the already vibrant Silk Road network and encouraging foreign merchants, including the famous Venetian explorer Marco Polo, to visit his empire.

Kublai Khan's reign brought a period of relative stability and prosperity to China and Mongolia, though it also saw the beginning of challenges that would eventually weaken the Yuan Dynasty. While Kublai had successfully unified China, he struggled to maintain control over the wider Mongol Empire, particularly in the west, where the Golden Horde, Ilkhanate, and Chagatai Khanate operated with increasing independence.

YUAN DYNASTY ADMINISTRATION (1294 – 1368)

After Kublai Khan's death in 1294, the Yuan Dynasty continued to rule over China for another seven decades, though it faced growing internal and external challenges. The Yuan administration, under Kublai's successors, was characterised by efforts to balance Mongol and Chinese cultural and political systems. Mongol rulers continued to occupy the highest positions in the government and military, but they relied heavily on Chinese officials to administer local governance and manage the economy.

One of the most significant aspects of Yuan administration was the integration of Mongol and Chinese cultural elements. Kublai Khan and his successors promoted the exchange of ideas, technologies, and religious practices between the Mongol heartlands and China. Mongol rulers were generally tolerant of religious diversity, and under their rule, Buddhism, Daoism, Islam, and Christianity flourished alongside traditional Chinese Confucianism. This cultural blending was also evident in art and architecture, as Mongol influences could be seen in Chinese artistic styles, while Chinese cultural practices influenced the Mongol court.

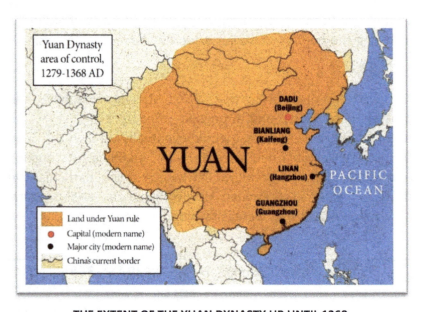

Yuan Dynasty area of control, 1279-1368 AD

YUAN

DADU (Beijing)
BIANLIANG (Kaifeng)
LINAN (Hangzhou)
GUANGZHOU (Guangzhou)

PACIFIC OCEAN

Land under Yuan rule
Capital (modern name)
Major city (modern name)
China's current border

THE EXTENT OF THE YUAN DYNASTY UP UNTIL 1368

Economically, the Yuan Dynasty was a period of growth and prosperity, largely due to the expansion of the Silk Road and the promotion of international trade. The Pax Mongolica, established under Genghis Khan, facilitated the movement of goods, people, and ideas across Eurasia, and under the Yuan, China became a vital part of this vast network. Trade routes connecting China to Persia, Central Asia, and Europe thrived, bringing luxury goods such as silk, porcelain, and tea to foreign markets. The Yuan Dynasty also developed a sophisticated postal and road system, which allowed for efficient communication across the empire.

However, despite these achievements, the Yuan Dynasty faced significant challenges. Kublai's successors were less capable rulers, and internal divisions within the Mongol elite led to factionalism and political instability. The Mongols struggled to maintain control over a vast and diverse empire, and their reliance on Chinese officials sometimes alienated their own Mongol supporters. In addition, the heavy taxation required to support the military and bureaucracy placed a strain on the peasantry, leading to widespread unrest and rebellion.

The Black Death, which swept through Asia and Europe in the mid-14th century, also severely impacted the Yuan Dynasty. The epidemic decimated the population, leading to labour shortages, economic decline, and further weakening the Mongol grip on power. As internal strife increased, rebellions erupted across China, including the Red Turban Rebellion, which would eventually bring about the dynasty's fall.

THE FALL OF THE YUAN (1368)

By the mid-14th century, the Yuan Dynasty was in a state of decline. The combination of internal power struggles, economic problems, and widespread dissatisfaction among the Chinese population created an environment ripe for rebellion. The most significant of these uprisings was led by Zhu Yuanzhang, a peasant who rose to prominence as a military leader during the Red Turban Rebellion.

Zhu's forces, drawing support from disaffected peasants, scholars, and military leaders, gradually gained control over large parts of China. In 1368, Zhu's army captured Khanbaliq, forcing

41

the last Yuan emperor, Toghon Temür, to flee north into Mongolia. This marked the end of the Yuan Dynasty in China and the beginning of the Ming Dynasty, which would rule China for nearly three centuries.

BATTLE BETWEEN MONGOL WARRIORS AND THE CHINESE

The fall of the Yuan Dynasty did not mark the complete end of Mongol power, however. In Mongolia, the remnants of the Yuan royal family and their supporters established the Northern Yuan, continuing to claim the title of Great Khan and ruling over the Mongol heartlands. While the Mongols never again ruled China, they remained a formidable force in Central and Inner Asia, and the legacy of the Yuan Dynasty continued to shape Mongol identity and governance for generations.

SUMMARY:

The preceding chapter introduced the remarkable yet challenging era when the Mongols, led by Kublai Khan, ruled China as the Yuan Dynasty. This chapter explored the fusion of Mongol and Chinese customs under foreign rule, a time marked by attempts at integration and, often, resistance. The Yuan era was a complex period of administration and adaptation, as Mongols strove to balance their nomadic traditions with the sophisticated demands of Chinese governance. Ultimately, these tensions would lead to the dynasty's collapse, a dramatic turning point in Mongolian and Chinese history.

DID YOU KNOW?

Kublai Khan, founder of the Yuan Dynasty, was a strategic thinker and an avid player of 'xiangqi' (Chinese chess). He reportedly used the game to illustrate battle strategies to his generals, blending his Mongolian heritage with Chinese tactical concepts, symbolising the cultural synthesis of the Yuan era.

PEOPLE

Kublai Khan (1215 – 1294) - The founder of the Yuan Dynasty and a grandson of Genghis Khan, Kublai Khan is one of Mongolia's most significant historical figures. He completed the conquest of China and established the Yuan Dynasty in 1271, ruling as its first emperor. Kublai expanded Mongol influence, embraced Chinese culture, and promoted trade across Asia, but his reign also marked the beginning of the Mongols' transition from nomadic to more sedentary rulers.

Chabi (c. 1225 – 1281) - Empress Chabi, the wife of Kublai Khan, was an influential figure during the early Yuan Dynasty. She played a key role in Kublai's court, advising him on matters of governance and diplomacy, particularly regarding religious tolerance and relations with China's Buddhist and Daoist communities. Her influence helped shape Kublai's policies of cultural accommodation.

Toghon Temür (1320 – 1370) - The last emperor of the Yuan Dynasty, Toghon Temür's reign saw the decline and eventual collapse of Mongol rule in China. Struggling with internal corruption, natural disasters, and the rise of peasant rebellions such as the Red Turban Rebellion, Toghon Temür's leadership was insufficient to maintain Mongol control, and he was eventually forced to flee north as the Ming Dynasty took power.

PLACES

Khanbaliq (Present-day Beijing, established in 1267) - Khanbaliq, also known as Dadu, was established by Kublai Khan as the capital of the Yuan Dynasty. It became the political and cultural centre of the Mongol Empire in China. The city was designed to reflect both Mongol and Chinese influences, serving as a symbol of Kublai's power and his attempt to integrate Mongol rule into Chinese traditions.

Shangdu (Summer Capital, founded in 1256) - Also known as Xanadu, Shangdu was the summer capital of the Yuan Dynasty. It was a luxurious retreat for the Mongol court, reflecting the nomadic heritage of the Mongols while also incorporating Chinese architectural styles. The city became legendary due to its depiction in literature, such as Samuel Taylor Coleridge's famous poem, "Kubla Khan."

Tibet (Subjugated in the 1270s) - Under Kublai Khan, Tibet was brought under Mongol control, making it a significant region within the Yuan Empire. Kublai appointed Tibetan lamas to important positions in the Yuan court, ensuring the spread of Tibetan Buddhism in Mongolia and strengthening ties between the Mongol rulers and the Tibetan religious elite.

EVENTS

Founding of the Yuan Dynasty (1271) - Kublai Khan declared the establishment of the Yuan Dynasty in 1271, marking the official Mongol rule over China. This event integrated the Mongol Empire into Chinese governance, blending Mongol and Chinese cultures. The founding of the Yuan Dynasty was also an important milestone in Mongolian history, symbolising the height of Mongol power in East Asia.

Conquest of the Southern Song Dynasty (1276 – 1279) - The Mongol victory over the Southern Song Dynasty marked the completion of Kublai Khan's conquest of China. The fall of the Song capital, Lin'an, in 1276 and the subsequent defeat of the last Song loyalists in 1279 solidified the Yuan Dynasty's control over the entirety of China, creating the first unified Chinese empire under foreign rule.

Promotion of the Pax Mongolica (1270s – 1300s) - Under Kublai Khan and his successors, the Yuan Dynasty promoted the Pax Mongolica, a period of stability and peace across the Mongol Empire. Trade flourished along the Silk Road, connecting East Asia with Europe and the Middle East. This era of open trade allowed for cultural exchange and economic growth, boosting the wealth and influence of the Yuan court.

Red Turban Rebellion (1351 – 1368) - The Red Turban Rebellion was a major peasant uprising that contributed to the collapse of the Yuan Dynasty. Discontent with high taxes, government corruption, and natural disasters, rebels challenged Mongol rule across China. The rebellion gained momentum under leaders like Zhu Yuanzhang, who eventually founded the Ming Dynasty in 1368, forcing the Yuan rulers to flee to the north.

The Fall of the Yuan Dynasty (1368) - The Yuan Dynasty's collapse in 1368, marked by the rise of the Ming Dynasty, ended Mongol rule in China. The last Yuan emperor, Toghon Temür, retreated to the Mongolian steppe, where his successors continued to rule as the Northern Yuan. The fall of the Yuan symbolised the Mongols' loss of control over China but allowed them to maintain influence in Mongolia for centuries to come.

CHAPTER 6

The Collapse of the Mongol Empire

1368 – 1600

END OF AN EMPIRE

*T*he collapse of the Mongol Empire was a gradual process that unfolded over the centuries following Genghis Khan's initial conquests. Although the Mongols had once ruled the largest contiguous empire in history, by the late 14th century, their power had significantly waned. The retreat of the Mongols to the steppe, following the rise of the Ming Dynasty in China, marked the beginning of a period of decline. Internal struggles, political fragmentation, and the rise of competing Mongol clans further contributed to the disintegration of Mongol unity, as they faced increasing challenges from both within and outside their borders. By the 16th century, the Mongol Empire was a shadow of its former self, with only remnants of their earlier power still visible on the steppe.

MING RESISTANCE AND MONGOL DECLINE (1368 – 1400)

The Ming Dynasty's rise to power in 1368, under the leadership of Zhu Yuanzhang, marked a significant turning point in the history of the Mongol Empire. The Ming successfully expelled the last Yuan emperor from China, forcing the Mongols to retreat to their homeland in the northern steppe. This marked the end of Mongol rule over China, but not the end of the Mongol presence in the region. After their expulsion, the Mongols reorganised themselves as the Northern Yuan Dynasty and continued to pose a threat to the Ming in the early years of the new dynasty.

The Ming rulers, however, were determined to prevent a Mongol resurgence. Ming emperors, particularly the Hongwu Emperor and his successors, launched a series of military campaigns aimed at neutralising the Mongol threat. These campaigns focused on defending the northern borders of China and preventing the Mongols from regrouping. The Ming fortified the Great Wall, reinforcing it as a defensive structure against the nomadic Mongols, whose hit-and-run tactics had been a hallmark of their military strategy for centuries.

PORTRAIT OF BILIGTÜ KHAN

While the Ming successfully repelled many Mongol incursions, they faced a constant challenge in managing the volatile northern frontier. The Mongols, under the leadership of various khans, made periodic attempts to reclaim their former power in China. One of the most notable of these efforts was the campaign led by the Mongol leader Toghon Temür's son, Biligtü Khan, who sought to reassert Mongol authority over northern China. However, internal divisions among the Mongol nobility and the strength of the Ming military ultimately thwarted these efforts.

Throughout this period, the Ming employed a combination of military force and diplomacy to manage the Mongol threat. They engaged in strategic alliances with various Mongol factions, playing one group off against another to prevent the reformation of a unified Mongol empire. By the end of the 14th century, the Mongols had largely been contained to the steppe, and their political and military influence in China had significantly diminished.

MONGOLIA'S INTERNAL STRUGGLES (1400 – 1600)

While the Ming Dynasty worked to weaken the Mongols from the south, the Mongols themselves were experiencing significant internal turmoil. The once unified empire had long since fragmented into competing factions, and by the 15th and 16th centuries, Mongolia was a patchwork of rival clans, each vying for supremacy. These internal divisions were exacerbated by the lack of a strong central authority, as no single khan was able to unite the disparate Mongol tribes under one banner.

The collapse of Mongol unity was partly a result of the political structure of the empire itself. Genghis Khan's descendants had divided the empire into khanates, each ruled by a branch of the Mongol royal family. While this system allowed for the efficient administration of vast territories, it also sowed the seeds of future conflict, as rival claimants to power emerged from different branches of the family. The Chinggisid principle of shared rule often led to disputes over succession, further weakening the Mongols' ability to maintain a cohesive state.

The Oirat and Eastern Mongol clans were two of the most prominent groups in this period of Mongol history. The Oirats, a powerful confederation of western Mongol tribes, rose to prominence in the 15th century and became a dominant force in Mongolian politics. Under leaders such as Esen Taishi, the Oirats challenged the authority of the Eastern Mongols and the Northern Yuan Dynasty. Esen, in particular, posed a significant threat to the Ming Dynasty as well, even capturing the Ming emperor during a battle in 1449, in what became known as the Tumu Crisis. However, despite their momentary successes, the Oirats were ultimately unable to unify the Mongols under their rule.

Meanwhile, the Eastern Mongols, based around the remnants of the Northern Yuan Dynasty, also struggled to maintain their authority. The khans of the Northern Yuan continued to claim the title of Great Khan, but their power was limited to their strongholds in the Mongolian steppe. They faced constant challenges from rival Mongol factions, and their attempts to rebuild the Mongol Empire were continually undermined by internal divisions.

By the 16th century, Mongolia had become a battleground for competing clans, each of which sought to assert its dominance. This period saw the rise of powerful local rulers, or taishis, who commanded the loyalty of various Mongol tribes. These rulers often formed temporary alliances to achieve their goals but were equally quick to break these alliances when it suited them. The result was a period of almost constant warfare and instability, with no single leader able to unify the Mongols.

The introduction of Tibetan Buddhism to Mongolia in the late 16th century provided some stability to the region. Altan Khan, one of the most prominent Mongol rulers of the time, embraced Buddhism and formed a close alliance with the Tibetan spiritual leader, the Dalai Lama. This alliance helped to spread Buddhism throughout Mongolia and provided a unifying cultural and religious identity for the Mongol people. However, while Buddhism helped to moderate the internal conflicts, it did not bring an end to the political fragmentation that had characterised Mongol society for over two centuries.

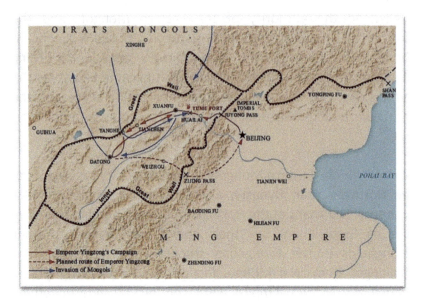

MAP SHOWING THE TUMU FORTRESS CRISIS OF THE MING DYNASTY

SUMMARY:

Building on the Yuan Dynasty's eventual decline, this chapter covered the final dissolution of the Mongol Empire, a slow fragmentation that saw Mongol power eroded by internal conflicts and external forces. The once-unified empire was now divided into smaller states, each adjusting to new challenges as regional influences began to reshape former Mongol territories. The end of this era marked a loss of centralised Mongol authority but left a cultural and political legacy that would resonate across Asia, as local leaders adapted Mongol customs and governance to their own realms.

DID YOU KNOW?

As the Mongol Empire fragmented, Mongolian folklore began to reflect a sense of foreboding and regret. Legends emerged that the spirit of Genghis Khan haunted those who allowed the empire to fall, instilling a cultural memory of accountability and reverence for the founder's legacy.

PEOPLE

Toghon Temür (1320 – 1370) - The last emperor of the Yuan Dynasty, Toghon Temür, ruled from 1333 until the Mongol Empire's collapse in China in 1368. His reign was marked by internal strife, corruption, and failed attempts to reform the weakening empire. His defeat by Zhu Yuanzhang, the founder of the Ming Dynasty, marked the end of Mongol rule in China and the loss of the empire's most significant territory.

Esen Taishi (1407 – 1455) - A powerful Oirat leader, Esen unified much of Mongolia and even captured the Ming Emperor in 1449 at the Battle of Tumu. Though his military success briefly revived Mongol strength, his assassination in 1455 led to further internal disunity and fragmentation among the Mongol factions.

Dayan Khan (1464 – 1543) - Dayan Khan revitalised the Mongol Empire after centuries of fragmentation. He reunified the Eastern and Western Mongols and established a centralised government. His efforts helped to stabilise Mongolia for a time, allowing the empire to fend off Chinese and Oirat pressures. However, his successors struggled to maintain unity.

PLACES

Khanbaliq (Present-day Beijing) - Khanbaliq, the capital of the Yuan Dynasty, was a significant Mongol power centre until the fall of the Yuan in 1368. The city's fall to the Ming forces marked the collapse of Mongol rule in China. It later became the capital of the Ming Dynasty, symbolising the end of Mongol dominance in East Asia.

Karakhoto (Abandoned in the late 14th century) - An important trade city on the Silk Road, Karakhoto was a vital outpost of the Western Mongol Empire. The city's decline in the late 14th century reflected the broader collapse of Mongol influence across Central Asia as internal conflicts and external pressures grew.

Ejin River Valley (c. 1400s – 1500s) - The Ejin River Valley, located in northern China and southern Mongolia, served as a refuge for Mongol factions after the fall of the Yuan Dynasty. As Mongol power waned, this region became a frontier zone where Mongol tribes regrouped, eventually becoming a base for leaders like Esen Taishi.

EVENTS

Fall of the Yuan Dynasty (1368) - The fall of the Yuan Dynasty in 1368, after more than a century of Mongol rule in China, marked the beginning of the Mongol Empire's fragmentation. The rise of the Ming Dynasty under Zhu Yuanzhang drove the Mongols out of China, forcing them to retreat to their homeland in the steppes and weakening their grip on other territories.

The Fragmentation of the Mongol Empire (1370s – 1400s) - After the Yuan Dynasty's fall, the Mongol Empire fractured into several competing khanates, including the Northern Yuan in Mongolia, the Chagatai Khanate in Central Asia, and the remnants of the Ilkhanate in Persia. These successor states struggled to maintain the unity and power once held by the united Mongol Empire.

Battle of Tumu (1449) - In a surprising victory, Esen Taishi, a Mongol leader of the Oirat, captured the Ming emperor in 1449. Although the battle was a significant victory for the Mongols, it did not lead to the re-establishment of a Mongol empire in China. Instead, Esen's assassination soon after led to further disunity among the Mongols, weakening their power.

Dayan Khan's Reunification (Early 16th Century) - Dayan Khan's efforts to reunify the Eastern and Western Mongols brought temporary stability to the Mongol heartlands after decades of internal strife. His reign saw a revival of Mongol military power and cultural identity, though his successors struggled to maintain this fragile unity after his death.

Decline of Mongol Power in Central Asia (Late 1500s) - By the late 16th century, the Mongol khanates had weakened due to internal divisions and external pressures from the rising powers of Russia, Persia, and the Ming Dynasty. The loss of key territories and the decline of their economic and military power marked the final stage in the collapse of the once-mighty Mongol Empire.

CHAPTER 7

Post-Mongol Empire to Qing Rule

1600 – 1911

Outer Mongolia — Khovd, Uliastai, Kyakhta, Küriye

Inner Mongolia — Hohhot

Qing dynasty

QING RULE SETS IN

*T*he period following the collapse of the Mongol Empire was marked by continued fragmentation and conflict among Mongol tribes. By the 17th century, the Mongols were divided primarily between two major groups: the

Oirat Mongols of the west and the Khalkha Mongols of the east. These two groups vied for control of the steppe, engaging in frequent wars and shifting alliances. As the power struggles between these Mongol factions intensified, an external force, the Qing Dynasty of China, began to exert its influence over Mongolia. By 1691, the Mongols had been brought under Qing control, marking the end of Mongol independence and the beginning of their incorporation into the Qing Empire. For over two centuries, Mongolian nobles played an important but subordinate role within the Qing administrative structure, preserving their status but losing much of their political autonomy.

THE OIRAT AND KHALKHA MONGOLS (1600 – 1691)

The 17th century was a tumultuous time for Mongolia, as the country was divided between the Oirat Mongols of the west and the Khalkha Mongols of the east. The Oirats, a confederation of western Mongol tribes, had risen to prominence in the 16th century and continued to be a powerful force in Central Asia. They were organised under leaders such as Khara Khula and his son, Galdan Boshugtu Khan, who sought to expand Oirat control over the Mongolian steppe and assert dominance over their eastern rivals, the Khalkha.

The Khalkha Mongols, on the other hand, represented the largest group of eastern Mongols. They were descendants of Genghis

Khan's eldest son, Jochi, and were traditionally based in northern and central Mongolia. The Khalkha were ruled by powerful noble families who traced their lineage directly back to Genghis Khan, and this connection to the imperial family gave them a strong sense of legitimacy and authority. However, the Khalkha were plagued by internal divisions, and their power was often undermined by competing clans and rivalries among their aristocracy.

GALDAN BOSHUGTU KHAN SELF-PROCLAIMED KHAN OF ALL MONGOLS

Throughout the 17th century, the Oirat and Khalkha Mongols were engaged in a series of conflicts over control of the steppe. These wars were driven by both political and economic factors, as the Mongols fought for dominance over vital grazing lands and trade routes. The Oirats, under the leadership of Galdan

Boshugtu Khan, launched several campaigns against the Khalkha in the 1670s and 1680s, attempting to unify Mongolia under Oirat rule. Galdan's ambition was to restore the unity of the Mongol Empire, and he proclaimed himself Khan of all Mongols in 1678. His military prowess and leadership earned him many followers, but his aggressive campaigns also alienated other Mongol factions, including the Khalkha.

The conflict between the Oirat and Khalkha Mongols culminated in a decisive confrontation in 1688, when Galdan's forces invaded Khalkha territory. The Khalkha Mongols, led by their chief, Zanabazar, were unable to withstand the Oirat onslaught and were forced to flee north into Russian Siberia. This marked the beginning of a period of intense instability in Mongolia, as the Khalkha sought external allies to help them resist Oirat domination. It was at this point that the Khalkha Mongols turned to the Qing Dynasty for assistance.

INCORPORATION INTO THE QING EMPIRE (1691 – 1911)

The Qing Dynasty, founded by the Manchus in 1644, was a rising power in East Asia. The Qing had already secured control over China and were looking to extend their influence into Mongolia and beyond. When the Khalkha Mongols appealed to the Qing for protection against the Oirats, the Qing Emperor Kangxi saw an opportunity to bring Mongolia under his control. In 1691, at the historic Dolon Nor Assembly, the Khalkha Mongols formally submitted to Qing authority, pledging loyalty to the emperor and agreeing to become subjects of the Qing Empire. This marked the beginning of Mongolia's incorporation into the Qing imperial system.

The Qing conquest of Mongolia did not end with the submission of the Khalkha. The Qing were determined to neutralise the Oirat threat as well, and in 1696, Kangxi launched a major military campaign against Galdan Boshugtu Khan. In a series of battles, the Qing forces decisively defeated the Oirats, and Galdan himself died in 1697, effectively ending Oirat ambitions for Mongol unification. The Qing subsequently brought the Oirat Mongols under their control, completing their domination of Mongolia.

A SCENE FROM THE QING'S SUCCESSFUL MILITARY CAMPAIGN AGAINST GALDAN BOSHUGTU KHAN IN 1696

Once Mongolia was integrated into the Qing Empire, the Qing government took steps to stabilise the region and consolidate its rule. The Mongol aristocracy, both Oirat and Khalkha, were incorporated into the Qing political system, where they were given titles and positions within the Qing administration. The

Qing employed a policy of indirect rule, allowing Mongolian nobles to maintain a degree of local autonomy, while ultimate authority rested with the Qing court. Mongolian khans and princes were granted noble ranks and privileges but were required to swear loyalty to the Qing emperor and serve as vassals of the empire.

The Qing also sought to manage Mongolia's internal divisions by imposing a system of administrative units known as 'banners' ('khoshuu'), which divided Mongol territory into distinct regions governed by local nobles. This system helped to prevent the re-emergence of powerful Mongol confederations that could challenge Qing authority. The Qing also maintained strict control over the military forces in Mongolia, ensuring that the Mongols could not form independent armies capable of rebellion.

Culturally, the Qing Dynasty promoted the spread of Tibetan Buddhism in Mongolia, seeing it as a means of pacifying the Mongol population. The Qing emperors themselves patronised Tibetan Buddhism, presenting themselves as protectors of the faith, and supported the building of monasteries and the promotion of Buddhist teachings throughout Mongolia. The Mongol nobles, who were deeply involved in Tibetan Buddhism, became important intermediaries between the Qing court and the Mongol people, using their religious authority to maintain their influence.

Under Qing rule, Mongolia remained largely isolated from the outside world. The Mongolian economy was heavily dependent on pastoralism, and the region saw little economic development during this period. Trade with China was strictly regulated, and the Qing imposed restrictions on the movement of Mongols, limiting their ability to engage in trade or migrate beyond their designated 'banners'. This isolation, combined with the relative stability provided by Qing rule, ensured that Mongolia remained a quiet frontier of the Qing Empire for much of the 18th and 19th centuries.

However, by the late 19th century, the Qing Dynasty was facing a series of internal crises, including economic decline, military defeats, and widespread rebellion. The weakening of the Qing state had significant implications for Mongolia, as the Mongols began to chafe under Qing rule and sought greater autonomy. This growing dissatisfaction would eventually lead to the Mongol independence movements of the early 20th century.

SUMMARY:

Our journey continued in this chapter, following Mongolia's path after the empire's fall. The absence of a centralised power allowed for intermittent independence, though Mongolia would eventually come under Qing Dynasty rule in the 17th century. The Qing's influence introduced new administrative systems that altered Mongolia's social and political landscape, leading to a period of reduced autonomy. This era saw Mongolians adapting to an imposed governance, an experience that profoundly impacted Mongolian society and set the stage for later independence efforts.

DID YOU KNOW?

By the time the Qing Dynasty absorbed Mongolia, the Under Qing rule, Mongolian wrestlers gained renown for their strength and skill, and some were even invited to the imperial court in China. Wrestling matches followed strict cultural customs; notably, each match was fought without time limits, and the losing wrestler had to remove his 'deel' (traditional garment) and leave the arena, marking a symbolic gesture of humility.

PEOPLE

Ligdan Khan (1588 – 1634) - The last significant ruler of the Northern Yuan Dynasty, Ligdan Khan attempted to reunify the Mongol tribes in the early 17th century. He struggled against the rising power of the Manchu, who would eventually establish the Qing Dynasty. Ligdan's defeat in 1634 by the Manchus marked the end of Mongol independence, as many Mongol tribes soon submitted to Qing authority.

Zanabazar (1635 – 1723) - A prominent religious leader and the first Jebtsundamba Khutuktu, Zanabazar was a key figure in Mongolian Buddhism. He worked to unify the Mongol tribes spiritually and culturally under Tibetan Buddhism and played a crucial role in maintaining Mongolian identity during Qing rule. His influence extended beyond religion, as he was involved in diplomacy with the Qing court.

Amursana (1723 – 1757) - A Mongol noble who initially collaborated with the Qing Empire, Amursana later rebelled against them in an attempt to restore Mongol independence. His uprising, known as the Dzungar Rebellion, was crushed by the Qing, leading to the fall of the Dzungar Khanate and further consolidation of Qing power over Mongolia.

PLACES

Khalkha (Northern Mongolia) - The Khalkha Mongols were a dominant group in northern Mongolia and played a central role in Mongolian politics during this era. Their allegiance to the Qing in 1691 at the Dolon Nor Assembly marked a significant shift, bringing large parts of Mongolia under Qing suzerainty. The Khalkha region became a key area of Qing control in Outer Mongolia.

Hohhot (Established 1580s) - Located in what is now Inner Mongolia, Hohhot became an important city for the Qing administration. The city grew under Qing rule as a hub of trade and military control over the region, especially during efforts to integrate the Mongols into the Qing Empire and promoted Tibetan Buddhism among the Mongols.

Erdene Zuu Monastery (Founded in 1585) - Built on the site of Genghis Khan's former capital of Karakorum, it became a significant centre of Mongolian Buddhism during the post-empire period symbolising the growing influence of Tibetan Buddhism. It was a focal point for Mongolian spiritual and cultural identity under Qing rule.

EVENTS

Submission of the Khalkha Mongols to the Qing (1691) - In 1691, the Khalkha Mongols, under increasing pressure from both the Dzungar Khanate and the rising Qing Empire, pledged allegiance to the Qing at the Dolon Nor Assembly. This marked the formal incorporation of Outer Mongolia into the Qing Empire, further solidifying Qing control over the Mongol territories.

Dzungar Rebellion and Qing Conquest (1755 – 1757) - The Dzungar Khanate, a Mongol kingdom in Western Mongolia, was the last significant Mongol power to resist Qing rule. Amursana's rebellion against the Qing ended in defeat, leading to the complete conquest of the Dzungars. The Qing's harsh suppression of the rebellion and subsequent campaigns effectively destroyed the Dzungar Khanate and secured Qing authority over the Mongol regions.

Rise of Tibetan Buddhism in Mongolia (17th – 18th Century) - The spread of Tibetan Buddhism throughout Mongolia, particularly through figures like Zanabazar, deeply influenced Mongolian society. The Qing actively supported Buddhism as a means of controlling the Mongols, using religious leaders to solidify their power. This religious revival helped maintain Mongolian culture and identity under foreign rule.

Mongolian Rebellions (1750s – 1800s) - Throughout the Qing era, various Mongol factions attempted to resist Qing rule, but most uprisings were quickly suppressed. Leaders like Amursana and Chingünjav led notable revolts, but their defeats only further entrenched Qing authority in Mongolia. These rebellions, however, symbolised ongoing Mongolian resistance to foreign domination.

Establishment of the Bogd Khanate (1911) - With the fall of the Qing Dynasty in 1911, Mongolia declared independence, establishing the Bogd Khanate under the leadership of the eighth Jebtsundamba Khutuktu, Bogd Khan. This marked the end of more than 200 years of Qing rule and the re-emergence of an autonomous Mongolian state, setting the stage for modern Mongolia's national identity and sovereignty.

CHAPTER 8

Mongolia in the Modern Era

1911 – 1921

THE WIND HORSE OF MONGOLIA

*T*he modern history of Mongolia is defined by its struggle for independence, first from the Qing Dynasty and later from competing foreign powers. At the beginning of the 20th century, Mongolia found itself in a period of transition, caught between the collapse of the Qing Empire *and the rising influence of revolutionary movements in Russia and China. The Mongolian people, long under the control of foreign rulers, sought to reassert their independence and establish a sovereign state. However, the road to freedom was far from simple. In the aftermath of the Qing collapse, Mongolia briefly established theocratic rule under the Bogd Khan, only to be drawn into the political turmoil of the Russian Revolution. This ushered in a new era of Soviet influence that would shape Mongolia's future for much of the 20th century.*

COLLAPSE OF THE QING (1911)

By the early 20th century, the Qing Dynasty, which had ruled China and its outer territories for over two centuries, was in a state of decline. Faced with internal rebellions, economic challenges, and pressure from foreign powers, the Qing government struggled to maintain control over its vast empire. Mongolia, which had been incorporated into the Qing system in 1691, was deeply affected by these developments. The Mongolian nobility, chafing under increasing Chinese influence and the decline of central Qing authority, began to look for opportunities to restore their independence.

The collapse of the Qing Dynasty in 1911 provided just such an opportunity. In October of that year, the Xinhai Revolution erupted in China, leading to the overthrow of the Qing and the establishment of the Republic of China. Sensing the fragility of Chinese control, Mongolian leaders quickly moved to declare independence. On December 29, 1911, Mongolia formally proclaimed its independence from China, establishing the Bogd Khanate, a theocratic state under the leadership of the eighth Jebtsundamba Khutuktu, who was enthroned as Bogd Khan, or "Holy King."

A YOUNG BOGD KHAN TO BE GREAT KHAN OF OUTER MONGOLIA

The Bogd Khanate was essentially a revival of the traditional Mongol theocracy, with the Bogd Khan serving as both the spiritual and political leader of the nation. The decision to establish a theocratic monarchy reflected the deep influence of Tibetan Buddhism in Mongolian society, particularly among the nobility. The Mongol aristocracy and Buddhist clergy played key roles in the movement for independence, viewing the collapse of the Qing as a chance to restore the autonomy of the Mongol people.

However, the declaration of independence was not immediately recognised by the new Republic of China, which still claimed Mongolia as part of its territory. The Chinese government, facing internal instability, lacked the means to reassert its control over the region, but it refused to accept Mongolia's secession. The international community, including the major powers of the time, also hesitated to recognise Mongolian independence, given the uncertain political situation in China.

Despite these challenges, the Bogd Khanate enjoyed a brief period of independence. The government, led by the Bogd Khan and supported by Mongolian nobles, sought to consolidate its authority over the country. However, the fledgling state lacked the military and economic resources to fully defend its sovereignty, and it soon found itself caught between larger regional powers.

Soviet Influence Begins (1911 – 1921)

While Mongolia's declaration of independence in 1911 marked a significant step toward self-determination, the country's political future would be shaped by the events of the Russian Revolution and the rise of Soviet influence. Russia, Mongolia's northern neighbour, had long played a role in Mongolian affairs. During the final years of the Qing Dynasty, Tsarist Russia had supported

Mongolia's autonomy in exchange for influence in the region. However, the collapse of the Russian Empire in 1917 and the subsequent Russian Civil War would have profound implications for Mongolia.

As the Russian Revolution unfolded, Mongolia's strategic position between Russia and China became increasingly important. In 1919, the Chinese government, under the control of warlord Duan Qirui, attempted to reassert its authority over Mongolia by sending military forces into the region. The Chinese occupation, however, was deeply unpopular among the Mongolian people, who had grown accustomed to their brief period of independence under the Bogd Khan. Resistance to Chinese rule grew, and many Mongolians looked to the Soviet Union, which had emerged as the dominant power in Russia, for support.

EMBLEM OF THE MONGOLIAN PEOPLE'S PARTY (MPP)

The Soviet Union, under Lenin's leadership, viewed Mongolia as a potential ally and buffer state against both China and Western powers. Soviet leaders were also sympathetic to the Mongolian independence movement, seeing it as part of the broader global struggle against imperialism. In 1920, the Soviet-backed Mongolian People's Party (MPP) was formed, with the goal of expelling the Chinese forces and establishing a new, socialist-oriented government in Mongolia.

In 1921, a coalition of Mongolian revolutionaries, led by Damdin Sükhbaatar, and supported by Soviet troops, launched a successful campaign to overthrow the Chinese occupation. The Mongolian People's Revolutionary Army, aided by Soviet military advisers, defeated the Chinese forces and entered the Mongolian capital of Urga (now Ulaanbaatar) in July 1921. The Chinese garrison surrendered, and the Bogd Khan was restored as a symbolic figurehead, although real power now lay with the MPP and its Soviet backers.

The revolution of 1921 marked the beginning of Mongolia's transformation into a socialist state under Soviet influence. Although the Bogd Khan retained his title as the spiritual leader of Mongolia until his death in 1924, the real political power shifted to the MPP, which pursued a radical agenda of land reform, anti-feudal policies, and the establishment of a socialist economy. The Soviet Union provided critical support to the new regime, helping to build its military, establish a centralised government, and develop infrastructure.

The relationship between Mongolia and the Soviet Union was solidified in the years that followed. Mongolia became a de facto Soviet satellite, with its political and economic policies closely aligned with those of the Soviet government. The country's leadership, including figures such as Sükhbaatar and Khorloogiin Choibalsan, looked to the Soviet Union as a model for building a socialist state. Soviet influence extended into all aspects of

Mongolian life, from education and industry to the military and foreign policy.

MONGOLIA'S LEADER DAMDIN SÜKHBAATAR IN 1921

SUMMARY:

The previous chapter examined Mongolia's quest for independence during the Qing decline, a struggle intensified by global shifts and regional conflicts in the early 20th century. Mongolia's growing desire for autonomy led to a wave of reform and self-assertion that laid the foundation for its modern identity. The chapter captured Mongolia's transformation from a territory

70

under foreign rule to a nation increasingly determined to shape its own future, an evolution that would prove essential as the country navigated the next major shift towards the Soviet sphere.

DID YOU KNOW?

Mongolia's first European-style opera, 'Three Sad Hills', debuted in 1934, reflecting the blending of Mongolian themes with Western artistic forms. Conducted by an Italian maestro sent by the Soviet Union, the opera was a notable cultural event that fused Russian, Italian, and Mongolian influences during Mongolia's early modern period.

PEOPLE

Bogd Khan (1869 – 1924) - As the spiritual and political leader of Mongolia, Bogd Khan became the head of the Bogd Khanate after Mongolia declared independence from the Qing Dynasty in 1911. He was the eighth Jebtsundamba Khutuktu and served as a theocratic monarch until the revolution in 1921. His leadership symbolised the continued influence of Buddhism in Mongolia's governance during its brief period of independence.

Damdin Sükhbaatar (1893 – 1923) - A key military leader and revolutionary figure, Damdin Sükhbaatar played a central role in Mongolia's fight for independence from both the Chinese Republic and Russian White forces. He led the Mongolian Partisan Army during the 1921 revolution and is considered one of the founding fathers of modern Mongolia, often referred to as the "hero of the revolution."

Baron Roman von Ungern-Sternberg (1886 – 1921) - A Russian White Army officer and warlord, Ungern-Sternberg briefly occupied Mongolia in 1920–1921, attempting to restore the Bogd Khan to power and establish a pan-Mongol empire. His reign of terror was short-lived, as he was defeated and captured by Soviet-backed Mongolian forces in 1921, marking the end of his influence in the region.

PLACES

Urga (Present-day Ulaanbaatar) - The capital of Mongolia during this period, Urga was the political and religious centre of the country. It was home to Bogd Khan's palace and became the focal point of both the 1911 independence movement and the 1921 revolution. Renamed Ulaanbaatar in 1924, it remains the capital of modern Mongolia.

Khovd (Occupied 1912) - Khovd, a region in western Mongolia, was an important Qing military outpost. After the collapse of the Qing Dynasty, Mongolian forces recaptured Khovd from the Chinese in 1912, marking one of the first military successes of the new independent Mongolia. This victory further solidified Mongolia's break from Chinese control.

Kyakhta (Treaty Signed in 1915) - The Treaty of Kyakhta was signed between Mongolia, China, and Russia in 1915. The treaty granted Mongolia autonomy under Chinese suzerainty while recognising

Russian influence in the region. Though it fell short of full independence, it marked a key moment in Mongolia's struggle for self-determination during the tumultuous years after 1911.

EVENTS

Mongolian Independence from Qing Dynasty (1911) - In December 1911, Mongolia declared independence from the collapsing Qing Dynasty, establishing the Bogd Khanate with Bogd Khan as its leader. This event marked the first modern assertion of Mongolian sovereignty after centuries of foreign domination. However, Mongolia's independence was tenuous, with China and Russia vying for influence in the region.

Chinese Invasion of Mongolia (1919) - After the fall of the Qing, China attempted to reassert control over Mongolia in 1919. Chinese troops occupied Urga, and Mongolian autonomy was effectively dissolved. This occupation was deeply unpopular and set the stage for the Mongolian revolution that followed, as nationalist and revolutionary forces sought to end Chinese control.

Russian Civil War and Mongolian Involvement (1917 – 1920) - The Russian Civil War had a significant impact on Mongolia, as both Red and White Russian forces moved through the region. The Russian White Army, led by Baron Ungern-Sternberg, briefly controlled parts of Mongolia in 1920, while Soviet Russia supported Mongolian revolutionaries, eventually helping to establish a socialist state in 1921.

Mongolian Revolution of 1921 - With support from Soviet Russia, Mongolian revolutionary forces led by Sükhbaatar overthrew the Chinese-backed government and expelled Baron Ungern-Sternberg's forces. The revolution established the Mongolian People's Republic, ending the Bogd Khanate's theocratic rule and marking the beginning of Mongolia's socialist era, with close ties to the Soviet Union.

The Treaty of Kyakhta (1915) - Signed between Mongolia, China, and Russia, this treaty granted Mongolia limited autonomy while recognising Chinese suzerainty and Russian influence. Though it fell short of the full independence that Mongolian leaders desired, the treaty helped to maintain a fragile peace until China's invasion in 1919, which reignited the struggle for Mongolian sovereignty.

CHAPTER 9

Soviet Influence and the People's Republic of Mongolia

1921 – 1990

*The 20th century saw Mongolia undergo
profound political, social, and economic
transformations under the heavy influence of the
Soviet Union. Following the Mongolian*

Revolution of 1921, Mongolia rapidly shifted from a theocratic state to a communist regime, becoming one of the first socialist countries in the world outside the Soviet Union. For nearly seven decades, Mongolia was closely aligned with the USSR, its political and economic development steered by Soviet ideology and policies. This period saw the creation of the Mongolian People's Republic, a series of brutal purges in the 1930s, and Mongolia's strategic involvement in World War II. Throughout the Cold War, Mongolia remained a steadfast Soviet ally, but the dominance of the USSR came with both opportunities and challenges.

THE MONGOLIAN PEOPLE'S REPUBLIC (1924 – 1930s)

The death of the Bogd Khan in 1924 marked a turning point for Mongolia's political future. With the last vestiges of theocratic rule gone, Mongolia officially became a socialist state, declaring itself the Mongolian People's Republic (MPR) later that year. This marked the establishment of a communist regime, modelled directly on the Soviet Union. The Mongolian People's Revolutionary Party (MPRP), which had led the 1921 revolution, assumed full control of the government, with strong backing from the Soviet Union.

The new government swiftly embarked on a series of radical reforms designed to reshape Mongolian society along Marxist-Leninist lines. One of the primary goals was the redistribution of land and the dismantling of the traditional feudal system, which had long dominated Mongolia's political and economic structure. Land reforms were implemented in the late 1920s, aimed at breaking up the large estates of the nobility and Buddhist monasteries. The government also nationalised key industries and began efforts to collectivise agriculture, although these efforts met with resistance from nomadic herders, who were reluctant to give up their traditional way of life.

SÜKHBAATAR MEETS WITH LENIN, A POSTER OF RUSSIAN COMMUNIST PARTY

In addition to land reforms, the government sought to modernise Mongolia's economy and infrastructure, with significant assistance from the Soviet Union. The Soviets provided financial aid, technical expertise, and political guidance to help transform Mongolia transitioned into a modern socialist state by establishing roads, building factories, and pushing for the industrialisation of its predominantly pastoral economy. Educational and literacy programs expanded, with a strong focus on Soviet-style political education.

However, Soviet influence extended beyond economic development. The Soviet Union played a direct role in shaping Mongolia's political institutions and leadership. Mongolian leaders were closely monitored by Moscow, and Soviet advisers held significant sway over domestic policies. While the Mongolian government sought to strengthen its sovereignty, in reality, it operated as a satellite state of the USSR, with its decisions largely influenced by Soviet interests.

STALINIST PURGES (1930s – 1940)

The 1930s were a dark chapter in Mongolia's history, as the country was swept by a wave of political repression and purges under the influence of Joseph Stalin's regime in the Soviet Union. These purges were driven by both internal and external pressures, as Mongolian leaders sought to consolidate power and eliminate potential rivals, while also carrying out Moscow's directives to eliminate perceived threats to the socialist revolution.

The primary targets of the purges were Mongolia's traditional elites, particularly Buddhist monks and nationalist leaders. Buddhism had long been a central part of Mongolian identity, with monasteries serving as major landholders and centres of social and political influence. However, under the new socialist regime, Buddhism was seen as a relic of the feudal past and an obstacle to the full implementation of communist ideology.

In 1937, a brutal campaign was launched to eradicate Buddhism from Mongolian society. Thousands of monasteries were destroyed, and tens of thousands of monks were either executed or forcibly secularised. By the end of the purges, nearly all of Mongolia's Buddhist institutions had been wiped out, and the religion, which had once been the heart of Mongolian life, was effectively banned.

COMMUNISTS DESTROYED MANY MONASTERIES - ONGIIN KHIID MONASTERY IS SHOWN HERE

The political purges also targeted nationalist leaders and intellectuals who were seen as a threat to the regime. Many of those who had played key roles in the 1921 revolution were arrested and executed, accused of counter-revolutionary activities or of harbouring nationalist sentiments that could undermine Soviet control. Choibalsan, Mongolia's leader during this period and a close ally of Stalin, oversaw the purges, ensuring that anyone suspected of disloyalty to the communist cause was eliminated. The purges left a deep scar on Mongolian society, as thousands were killed, imprisoned, or exiled.

WORLD WAR II AND MONGOLIA'S ROLE (1941 – 1945)

During World War II, Mongolia found itself in a strategically important position as a Soviet ally. Although Mongolia did not directly engage in large-scale military operations, its role as a supplier of resources and support for the Soviet Union was critical. From the early 1940s, Mongolia provided significant material aid to the Soviet war effort, supplying horses, livestock, wool, and other essential goods. The Mongolian people contributed to Soviet campaigns financially as well, raising funds to support the Red Army. The "Revolutionary Mongolia" tank brigade, funded by Mongolian donations, was famously presented to the Soviet military.

COMMANDERS OF THE 6TH MONGOLIAN CAVALRY DIVISION, KHALKHIN GOL, AUGUST 1939

Mongolia's location between the Soviet Union and Japan also gave it strategic importance. The Soviets maintained a strong military presence in Mongolia, and the country served as a buffer zone against Japanese forces, who occupied parts of China. Mongolian troops, although not heavily involved in combat, played a supporting role in the Soviet-Japanese conflict. In the summer of 1945, as the war was drawing to a close, Mongolian forces participated in the Soviet invasion of Japanese-occupied

Manchuria, which helped hasten Japan's surrender and the end of the war in the Pacific.

Mongolia's contributions during the war strengthened its ties with the Soviet Union, and in the post-war years, Soviet influence over Mongolia would become even more pronounced.

THE COLD WAR ERA (1946 – 1990)

In the decades following World War II, Mongolia solidified its position as a loyal member of the Soviet bloc. The Cold War brought both opportunities and challenges for Mongolia, as the country became deeply intertwined with the USSR's geopolitical interests and economic system.

Mongolia's alignment with the Soviet Union during the Cold War led to increased economic assistance and infrastructure development. The Soviet Union invested heavily in Mongolia, helping to industrialise the country, modernise its transportation networks, and build up its education and healthcare systems. Soviet-style central planning was introduced, and Mongolia's economy became highly dependent on Soviet aid, with Moscow providing financial support, technical expertise, and machinery.

During the Cold War era, Mongolia's strategic significance also grew. The country served as a buffer state between the Soviet Union and China, particularly after the Sino-Soviet split in the 1960s. Mongolia's loyalty to the Soviet Union was rewarded with strong military and economic backing, but it also meant that the country was increasingly drawn into the global Cold War rivalry. However, Soviet domination came with significant challenges. Mongolia's political leadership remained tightly controlled by the Soviet Union, and the country had little autonomy in determining its own policies. The economy, while benefiting from Soviet investment, was heavily dependent on Soviet trade and aid, leaving Mongolia vulnerable to shifts in Soviet policy.

By the 1980s, as the Soviet Union began to face its own internal economic crises and political upheavals, Mongolia's dependence on the USSR became increasingly problematic. The eventual collapse of the Soviet Union in 1991 would bring an end to Mongolia's long-standing alliance with its northern neighbour, and the country would have to navigate a difficult transition to a market economy and a democratic political system.

RELATIONS BETWEEN MAO AND SOVIET LEADER NIKITA KHRUSHCHEV SOURED LEADING TO THE SINO-SOVIET SPLIT IN 1960

SUMMARY:

Building upon Mongolia's push for independence, the last chapter took us into the era of Soviet influence that fundamentally reshaped the nation. With the establishment of the People's Republic of Mongolia in 1924, the country adopted Communist policies and began a period of rapid industrialisation under Soviet guidance. Traditional structures gave way to collective agriculture and centralised governance, transforming Mongolian society. This period left an indelible mark, as Mongolia adapted Soviet-style reforms that shaped its political and social landscape for much of the 20th century.

DID YOU KNOW?

The Soviet-influenced Communist regime in Mongolia instituted a "wool quota," requiring citizens to produce or supply a fixed amount of wool each year, a policy designed to support the textile industry. Citizens unable to meet their quota could offer knitted goods or cash in its place, illustrating the collectivist approach to resource management.

PEOPLE

Khorloogiin Choibalsan (1895 – 1952) - Often referred to as Mongolia's Stalin, Choibalsan was the leader of the Mongolian People's Republic from the 1930s until his death in 1952. As a close ally of the Soviet Union, he implemented Stalinist policies, including collectivisation, purges of political rivals, and suppression of Buddhism. His rule was marked by Soviet-backed political repression but also industrial and educational reforms that modernised the country.

Yumjaagiin Tsedenbal (1916 – 1991) - Tsedenbal was Mongolia's longest-serving leader, governing from 1940 to 1984. A strong ally of the Soviet Union, he promoted socialist reforms and maintained a close relationship with Moscow throughout his tenure. His leadership saw significant industrial development and economic centralisation, though it was also characterised by increasing authoritarianism. Tsedenbal was removed from power in 1984 due to old age and Soviet pressure.

Jambyn Batmönkh (1926 – 1997) - Batmönkh was the leader of Mongolia during the final years of the People's Republic, serving as chairman of the People's Revolutionary Party from 1984 to 1990. He played a key role in the peaceful transition of Mongolia from socialism to democracy in 1990, stepping down without violence and allowing democratic reforms to take place.

PLACES

Ulaanbaatar (Capital of the People's Republic) - Ulaanbaatar, the capital of Mongolia, was the political, economic, and cultural centre of the Mongolian People's Republic. During Soviet influence, the city underwent rapid industrialisation and modernisation. Many Soviet-style buildings, industries, and infrastructure projects were established, transforming it into a hub of socialist development.

Khalkhin Gol (Site of 1939 Soviet-Japanese Conflict) - The Khalkhin Gol region, near the border of Mongolia and Manchukuo, was the site of a significant conflict between Soviet-Mongolian forces and the Japanese in 1939. The Battle of Khalkhin Gol, a decisive Soviet victory, secured Mongolia's borders and strengthened Soviet-Mongolian relations, marking a key moment in the region's history.

Choibalsan City (Formerly Bayan Tümen) - Renamed in honour of Khorloogiin Choibalsan in 1941, this city in eastern Mongolia was an important military and industrial centre during the Soviet era. It symbolised the deep ties between Mongolia and the Soviet Union and was a key location for Soviet influence in Mongolia's military and economic policies.

EVENTS

Mongolian Revolution of 1921 - The revolution, led by the Mongolian People's Party and backed by Soviet Russia, ousted the Chinese-backed government and established the Mongolian People's Republic. This marked the beginning of Soviet influence in Mongolia, with the country becoming a satellite state aligned with Soviet policies and ideology for the next seven decades.

The Purges of the 1930s - Under Choibalsan's rule, and with guidance from the Soviet Union, Mongolia experienced a series of political purges during the 1930s. Thousands of perceived enemies of the state, including Buddhist monks, aristocrats, and intellectuals, were executed or imprisoned. The purges helped solidify Soviet-style socialism and greatly weakened Mongolia's traditional religious and political institutions.

Battle of Khalkhin Gol (1939) - The Battle of Khalkhin Gol was a decisive confrontation between Soviet-Mongolian forces and the Japanese Kwantung Army. The Soviet victory, led by General Zhukov, secured Mongolia's independence from Japanese expansionism and solidified Soviet dominance in the region. It also ensured that Mongolia would remain within the Soviet sphere of influence during World War II.

Collectivisation of Agriculture (1950s) - In the 1950s, under Tsedenbal's leadership, Mongolia underwent a period of forced collectivisation, following the Soviet model. Nomadic herders were required to join collective farms, which transformed Mongolia's traditional pastoral economy. While the policy increased state control, it disrupted the nomadic lifestyle and created significant hardships for many Mongolians.

Mongolia's Role in the Cold War (1945 – 1989) - Throughout the Cold War, Mongolia was a key Soviet ally in East Asia. The country hosted Soviet military bases and was a buffer state between the USSR and China. Mongolia's strategic location made it important in Soviet defence policies, especially during the Sino-Soviet split, when Mongolia aligned firmly with Moscow.

Democratic Revolution of 1990 - In response to global political changes and economic stagnation, a peaceful revolution began in Mongolia in 1990. Protestors called for democratic reforms, leading to the resignation of the government and the adoption of a new constitution. This marked the end of the Mongolian People's Republic and the transition to a multi-party democratic system, with the first democratic elections held in 1992.

Soviet Economic Aid and Influence (1920s – 1980s) - For most of the 20th century, Mongolia's economy was heavily dependent on Soviet aid and trade. The Soviets helped build infrastructure, industries, and schools in Mongolia, transforming its largely agrarian society. However, this dependence left Mongolia vulnerable when Soviet support began to wane in the 1980s, contributing to the economic crisis that preceded the 1990 revolution.

CHAPTER 10

The End of the Cold War and Democratic Transition

1990 – PRESENT

END OF THE COLD WAR

*T*he end of the Cold War brought profound changes to Mongolia, as the collapse of the Soviet Union forced the country to re-evaluate its political and economic systems. For nearly seven decades, Mongolia had operated as a communist *tate closely aligned with the USSR, but by the late 1980s, the winds of change were blowing across Eastern Europe and Asia. Inspired by the political liberalisation sweeping through the Soviet bloc, Mongolians began to push for greater political freedom and reforms. In 1990, Mongolia experienced its own revolution—a peaceful, democratic transition that ended communist rule and ushered in a new era of democracy and economic reform.*

DEMOCRATIC REVOLUTION (1990)

The events of 1990 marked a turning point in Mongolian history. As the Soviet Union began to weaken under Mikhail Gorbachev's policies of 'perestroika' (restructuring) and 'glasnost' (openness), similar calls for reform emerged in Mongolia. Decades of economic stagnation, political repression, and dependency on the Soviet Union had left the country vulnerable, and many Mongolians—particularly the younger generation—were eager for change.

The Mongolian Democratic Revolution of 1990 was characterised by peaceful protests, hunger strikes, and public demonstrations in the capital, Ulaanbaatar. Protesters, led by students and intellectuals, demanded political reform, an end to one-party rule by the Mongolian People's Revolutionary Party (MPRP), and the establishment of a multi-party democracy. The demonstrations grew in size and influence, drawing support from various segments of society, including workers, professionals, and former political prisoners.

Under mounting pressure, the MPRP leadership, headed by Jambyn Batmönkh, agreed to engage in negotiations with the opposition and initiated political reforms. In March 1990, Batmönkh and the Politburo resigned, paving the way for democratic elections. The first multi-party elections were held in July 1990, marking the official end of one-party communist rule in Mongolia. While the MPRP won a majority of seats, opposition parties gained representation, and a new democratic constitution was adopted in 1992. This established Mongolia as a parliamentary republic, with free elections, political pluralism, and protection of civil liberties.

Mongolia's peaceful transition from communism to democracy was notable for its lack of violence and upheaval, a contrast to the often bloody revolutions that took place elsewhere in the post-Soviet world. The revolution also signified the beginning of a new era in Mongolian politics, one marked by democratic governance and increasing engagement with the international community.

MAINLY PEACEFUL PROTESTS FOR DEMOCRACY IN 1990

While Mongolia's democratic transition was successful, the country faced significant challenges in the 1990s as it sought to reform its economy and navigate the post-communist world. Mongolia's economy had been heavily dependent on Soviet aid, which accounted for a large portion of its industrial output, trade, and infrastructure development. With the collapse of the Soviet Union in 1991, Mongolia lost its main economic partner and was plunged into a severe economic crisis.

The early years of transition were marked by efforts to shift from a centrally planned economy to a market-based system. Economic liberalisation policies were implemented, including the privatisation of state-owned enterprises, land reforms, and the liberalisation of trade. However, these reforms were not without difficulty. The rapid transition to a market economy led to widespread unemployment, inflation, and a decline in living standards for much of the population. Many state-owned industries, which had been dependent on Soviet subsidies, collapsed, and Mongolia struggled to attract foreign investment during the early years of reform.

The social impact of economic transition was also significant. Poverty rates increased, and the government faced challenges in providing adequate social services, healthcare, and education. However, despite these difficulties, Mongolia persevered in its efforts to establish a functioning market economy, and by the 2000s, the country began to experience steady economic growth.

Alongside economic reforms, Mongolia also saw a resurgence in traditional culture and religion during this period. The fall of communism allowed for the revival of Mongolian Buddhism, which had been suppressed during the Soviet era. Monasteries were rebuilt, religious practices were once again embraced, and

Mongolian identity, rooted in its nomadic and Buddhist heritage, was revitalised. The revival of traditional culture became an important part of Mongolia's national identity in the post-communist era, helping to unify the country during a time of economic uncertainty.

Politically, Mongolia also faced the challenge of building stable democratic institutions. The 1990s saw the development of a vibrant, multi-party political system, with the MPRP and opposition parties alternating in power. Corruption, however, remained an issue, and there were concerns about the effectiveness of governance and the rule of law. Nonetheless, Mongolia's commitment to democratic principles and the peaceful transfer of power set it apart from many other former communist states.

MONGOLIA'S ROLE IN INTERNATIONAL AFFAIRS (2000S – PRESENT)

In the 21st century, Mongolia has emerged as a democratic state with an active role in international affairs. Mongolia's unique geopolitical position, sandwiched between two great powers—Russia and China—has required careful diplomacy as the country seeks to balance its relations with its neighbours while expanding ties with the broader international community.

Mongolia's foreign policy in the post-Cold War era has been characterised by a "third neighbour" strategy, aimed at reducing its dependence on Russia and China by strengthening relations with other countries, particularly in the West. Mongolia has forged strong ties with the United States, the European Union, Japan, and South Korea, among others. The country's democratic credentials have helped it gain support and recognition on the international stage, and Mongolia has been an active participant in international organisations, including the United Nations and the World Trade Organisation.

One of Mongolia's key contributions to global peace efforts has been its involvement in international peacekeeping missions. Since 2002, Mongolian soldiers have participated in UN peacekeeping operations in countries such as South Sudan, Sierra Leone, and Afghanistan. This involvement has not only strengthened Mongolia's international reputation but also provided valuable military experience and training for its armed forces.

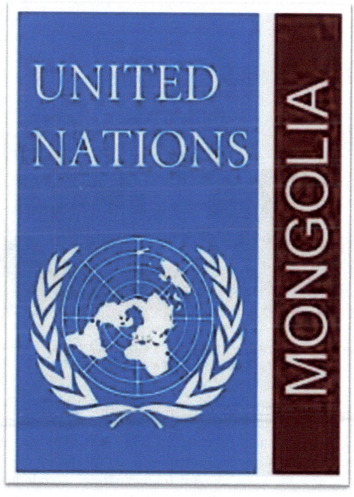

MONGOLIA AND ACTIVE PARTICIPANT IN THE UNITED NATIONS

Economically, Mongolia has experienced significant growth in the 21st century, largely driven by its vast natural resources. The country is rich in mineral resources, including coal, copper, gold, and uranium, and the mining sector has become a major contributor to the economy. Foreign investment, particularly from China, has poured into Mongolia's mining industry, leading to a period of rapid economic expansion in the 2000s and early 2010s. However, this growth has also made Mongolia vulnerable to fluctuations in global commodity prices, and the government has had to carefully manage the environmental and social impacts of mining.

U.S. PRESIDENT GEORGE W. BUSH MEETS MONGOLIAN PRIME MINISTER ELBEGDORJ IN ULAANBAATAR ON 2005

Mongolia's relations with its two powerful neighbours, Russia and China, have continued to evolve. While Mongolia maintains strong historical and cultural ties with Russia, its economic relationship with China has grown significantly in recent decades. China is now Mongolia's largest trading partner, accounting for the majority of its exports, particularly in the mining sector.

Mongolia's leaders have sought to maintain a delicate balance between Russia and China, seeking economic cooperation while guarding against becoming overly dependent on either power.

In recent years, Mongolia has also taken steps to strengthen its democracy and address issues such as corruption and political transparency. Former president Tsakhiagiin Elbegdorj played a significant role in promoting democratic reforms, advocating for transparency and accountability in governance. Under his leadership, electoral reforms were introduced to improve the fairness of elections, and efforts were made to curb corruption within government institutions. Despite these initiatives, Mongolia continues to face challenges related to governance and economic inequality.

SUMMARY:

Following the chapter on Soviet influence, we examined Mongolia's peaceful shift from Communism to democracy after the Cold War. In the early 1990s, Mongolia introduced political pluralism and market reforms, initiating a remarkable transformation into a democratic state. The transition was not without challenges, but Mongolia embraced new freedoms and established its identity as a democratic nation amid regional powers. This era marked a historic turning point, as Mongolia redefined itself on the world stage, guided by a commitment to democratic values and self-determination.

DID YOU KNOW?

During Mongolia's transition to democracy in the early 1990s, candidates sometimes adopted the name "Chinggis Khan" for campaign purposes, aiming to invoke the revered founder's legacy to garner public support. This strategy, however, gave way to a more serious focus on reform and policy, as voters began prioritising democratic ideals over symbolic references.

PEOPLE

Punsalmaagiin Ochirbat (b. 1942) - Ochirbat was the first president of Mongolia after the democratic revolution of 1990. As a reform-minded leader, he played a pivotal role in guiding Mongolia through its peaceful transition from a socialist state to a democratic republic. Elected as president in 1993, Ochirbat oversaw the drafting of Mongolia's new democratic constitution and the country's shift toward a market economy.

Nambaryn Enkhbayar (b. 1958) - Enkhbayar served as prime minister (2000–2004), president (2005–2009), and was a key figure in Mongolia's post-socialist political landscape. He played a significant role in stabilising the economy and pursuing a balanced foreign policy between Russia, China, and the West. His presidency was marked by both reforms and accusations of corruption, leading to his later imprisonment in 2012.

Tsakhiagiin Elbegdorj (b. 1963) - A leading figure in the 1990 democratic revolution, Elbegdorj served as Mongolia's prime minister twice (1998 and 2004–2006) and later as president (2009–2017). A strong advocate for democracy, human rights, and free markets, he spearheaded Mongolia's participation in global organisations like the UN and expanded ties with Western countries, enhancing Mongolia's international profile.

PLACES

Sükhbaatar Square (Ulaanbaatar) - Renamed Chinggis Square in 2013, this central square in Ulaanbaatar is where the democratic protests of 1990 took place. It became a symbol of Mongolia's democratic movement and remains an important political and cultural landmark in the country, hosting national celebrations and political events.

Oyu Tolgoi (Discovered 2001) - Located in the Gobi Desert, Oyu Tolgoi is one of the largest copper and gold mines in the world. Its discovery and subsequent development in the early 21st century significantly boosted Mongolia's economy, attracting foreign investment and establishing mining as a key industry. However, it has also sparked debates over resource management and economic inequality.

Khuraldai Hall (Parliament Building, Ulaanbaatar) - As the seat of Mongolia's legislative body, the State Great Khural, Khuraldai Hall is where the country's democratic laws and reforms have been debated and passed since 1990. It serves as a key symbol of Mongolia's parliamentary democracy, hosting national and international political discussions.

EVENTS

Democratic Revolution of 1990 - In early 1990, peaceful protests, spearheaded by students and intellectuals, demanded political and economic reforms in Mongolia. The ruling Communist Party eventually relinquished power, leading to the establishment of a multi-party system. This revolution marked the end of one-party socialist rule and the beginning of Mongolia's transition to democracy.

Adoption of the New Constitution (1992) - In 1992, Mongolia adopted a new democratic constitution, replacing the socialist-era document. The new constitution guaranteed human rights, established a multi-party system, and defined Mongolia as a democratic republic. It also laid the foundation for the separation of powers, creating a parliamentary system with an elected president and legislative body.

First Democratic Elections (1992) - Mongolia held its first democratic parliamentary elections in 1992 under the new constitution, marking a major milestone in the country's transition to democracy. The former communist party, now renamed the Mongolian People's Revolutionary Party (MPRP), won the election, but the multiparty system allowed for a more pluralistic political landscape to develop.

Oyu Tolgoi Mining Agreement (2009) - The 2009 agreement between Mongolia and international companies to develop the Oyu Tolgoi mine was a turning point for the country's economy. The deal attracted significant foreign investment and made Mongolia one of the fastest-growing economies in the early 2010s. However, it also sparked debates about resource management and the distribution of mining profits.

Mongolian Economic Boom and Slowdown (2010s) - Fuelled by the development of its mining sector, Mongolia experienced rapid economic growth in the early 2010s, becoming one of the world's fastest-growing economies. However, the economic boom was followed by a slowdown due to fluctuating commodity prices, political instability, and challenges in managing foreign investment, particularly in the mining sector.

Corruption Scandals and Political Reform (2000s – 2010s) - Mongolia's post-socialist political system faced numerous corruption scandals, involving high-profile politicians such as Nambaryn Enkhbayar. These scandals led to growing public dissatisfaction and calls for greater transparency and political reform, which have shaped the country's ongoing democratic development.

Foreign Policy Balancing (1990 – Present) - Since the 1990s, Mongolia has pursued a foreign policy aimed at balancing relations with its two powerful neighbours, Russia and China, while also strengthening ties with Western nations, Japan, and South Korea. Known as the "Third Neighbour Policy," this approach has helped Mongolia maintain independence and diversify its international partnerships, particularly in trade and diplomacy.

COVID-19 Pandemic and Economic Impact (2020s) - Like much of the world, Mongolia was significantly impacted by the COVID-19 pandemic, facing economic disruptions due to its dependence on trade and mining. The government implemented strict lockdown measures to control the spread of the virus. The pandemic also underscored the need for economic diversification beyond the mining sector.

Rise of Civil Society and Environmental Movements (2000s – Present) - In recent years, civil society organisations and environmental movements have gained prominence in Mongolia. They focus on issues like pollution, desertification, and the effects of mining on traditional nomadic lifestyles. These groups have increasingly influenced national policies and fostered greater public participation in Mongolia's democracy.

2021 Presidential Election - The 2021 presidential election marked a shift in Mongolia's political landscape, with the newly formed Mongolian People's Party (MPP) winning both the presidency and parliamentary control. This has created concerns over the concentration of political power, though the government continues to uphold democratic principles amidst the evolving political dynamics.

CHAPTER 11

Mongolia Today

PRESENT TIME

MONGOLIA TODAY

In the 21st century, Mongolia stands at a crossroads, navigating the challenges and opportunities of balancing its rich cultural heritage with the demands of modernisation. Following the collapse of communism and the democratic transition of the 1990s, Mongolia has experienced significant changes in its social, *economic, and environmental landscape. While the country has achieved remarkable economic growth and urban development, it also faces complex issues such as the preservation of its traditional nomadic culture and the growing impact of climate change. Mongolia's path forward is defined by its efforts to maintain this delicate balance between tradition and modernity.*

CULTURAL REVIVAL (1990 – PRESENT)

Since the fall of the communist regime in 1990, Mongolia has undergone a profound cultural revival, as the nation reclaims its identity after decades of Soviet influence. Central to this revival has been a renewed emphasis on preserving the Mongolian language, arts, religion, and the traditional nomadic lifestyle that has been the heart of the country's identity for centuries.

The Mongolian language, which was historically marginalised during the communist era, has experienced a resurgence in national pride and importance. Efforts have been made to strengthen the use of Mongolian in education, government, and media, and to promote its rich literary heritage. This includes a focus on reviving classical Mongolian script, which had been replaced by the Cyrillic alphabet under Soviet influence. Today, classical script is taught in schools and used in official documents, symbolising Mongolia's commitment to its linguistic roots.

Mongolia's artistic and cultural scene has also flourished in recent decades. The revival of traditional music, dance, and crafts has been a major focus of national pride. Mongolian throat singing ('khoomei'), horsehead fiddle music ('morin khuur'), and traditional folk dances have regained prominence, with cultural festivals and performances celebrating these ancient arts. The preservation of nomadic craftsmanship, such as felt-making and the construction of traditional 'ger' (yurts), also remains a vital link to Mongolia's past.

THE REVIVAL OF CLASSICAL MONGOLIAN SCRIPT

One of the most significant aspects of Mongolia's cultural revival is the resurgence of Buddhism, which had been severely repressed during the communist era. Since the 1990s, monasteries have been rebuilt, religious freedoms have been restored, and Mongolian Buddhism has once again become a cornerstone of national identity. The re-establishment of the Buddhist faith, alongside Mongolia's shamanistic traditions, has contributed to the country's spiritual and cultural revival.

At the heart of Mongolia's cultural heritage is its nomadic way of life, which continues to be a defining feature of the nation's identity. For centuries, Mongolians have lived as herders, moving across the vast steppe in search of pasture for their livestock. Despite the pressures of modernisation and urbanisation, a significant portion of Mongolia's population remains nomadic or semi-nomadic. In recent years, the government and various organisations have made concerted efforts to preserve and promote this way of life. Programmes have been introduced to support nomadic communities, including initiatives to improve access to education, healthcare, and infrastructure for herders.

PRESERVATION OF MONGOLIAN TRADITIONAL NOMADIC LIFESTYLE

However, preserving the nomadic way of life in the face of rapid urbanisation presents challenges. Many young Mongolians are moving to cities, particularly the capital Ulaanbaatar, in search of education and economic opportunities. This migration has led to concerns about the future of the nomadic tradition, as the younger generation becomes more disconnected from rural life. Balancing the preservation of this heritage with the demands of modern life remains a central challenge for Mongolia today.

ECONOMIC TRANSFORMATION (2000 – PRESENT)

Mongolia's economy has undergone a dramatic transformation in the 21st century, driven largely by the development of its vast mineral resources. The country is rich in natural resources, including coal, copper, gold, and rare earth minerals, which have attracted significant foreign investment and contributed to rapid economic growth. Mining has become the backbone of Mongolia's economy, accounting for a large share of its GDP and export earnings.

The development of large-scale mining projects, such as the Oyu Tolgoi copper and gold mine, has brought both opportunities and challenges. On one hand, the influx of foreign capital and the rise in commodity prices have fuelled economic expansion and contributed to the modernisation of Mongolia's infrastructure. Urban centres like Ulaanbaatar have experienced rapid growth, with new construction projects, modern amenities, and improved transportation networks transforming the cityscape.

However, Mongolia's reliance on mining has also made the economy vulnerable to fluctuations in global commodity prices. The boom-and-bust cycles of the mining sector have led to economic instability at times, as the country struggles to diversify its economy and reduce its dependence on resource extraction. Additionally, the benefits of mining have not always been evenly distributed, with concerns about inequality and the environmental impact of large-scale mining operations.

Urbanisation has been one of the most visible effects of Mongolia's economic transformation. Ulaanbaatar, the capital, has grown rapidly in recent decades, becoming home to nearly half of the country's population. The city's rapid growth has created challenges, including traffic congestion, pollution, and a housing shortage, particularly for the influx of rural migrants. The expansion of informal 'ger' districts on the outskirts of the city, where many former herders now live, has highlighted the socio-economic disparities between rural and urban populations.

ONE OF THE SHAFTS AT THE OYU TOLGOI COPPER AND GOLD MINE

Despite these challenges, Mongolia has made significant strides in modernising its economy and improving living standards. The country has invested in education, healthcare, and infrastructure, and continues to explore ways to diversify its economy beyond mining. The government has also sought to promote tourism, capitalising on Mongolia's unique cultural heritage and natural beauty as a way to generate income and create jobs.

As Mongolia continues to develop economically, it faces increasing environmental challenges, particularly in the context of climate change and desertification. Mongolia's fragile ecosystem, characterised by vast grasslands, deserts, and mountainous regions, is highly sensitive to environmental degradation. In recent years, climate change has exacerbated the pressures on Mongolia's environment, threatening the livelihoods of its nomadic herders and the sustainability of its natural landscapes.

Desertification is one of the most pressing environmental concerns in Mongolia. The expansion of the Gobi Desert, coupled with overgrazing and deforestation, has led to the degradation of large areas of pastureland. This process threatens the traditional nomadic way of life, as herders struggle to find adequate grazing land for their livestock. The increasing frequency of 'dzuds'—severe winters that lead to mass livestock deaths—has further compounded the challenges faced by rural communities. These harsh environmental conditions have pushed many herders to abandon their traditional way of life and migrate to urban areas, contributing to the growth of Ulaanbaatar's 'ger' districts.

Climate change has also had a significant impact on Mongolia's water resources. The melting of glaciers in the Altai Mountains and changing precipitation patterns have affected water availability, particularly in rural areas. The drying up of rivers and lakes poses a threat to both human populations and wildlife, and the scarcity of water has become a growing concern for the country's agricultural and Industrial sectors.

In response to these challenges, Mongolia has taken steps to address environmental degradation and protect its natural landscapes. The government has implemented policies aimed at combating desertification, including reforestation efforts, sustainable land management practices, and the establishment of protected areas. Mongolia has also been an active participant in international climate change initiatives, recognising the need for global cooperation to mitigate the effects of climate change.

Efforts to promote renewable energy have gained traction in recent years, as Mongolia seeks to reduce its reliance on coal and develop cleaner sources of energy. The country's vast potential for wind and solar power has attracted interest from both domestic and international investors, and there are ongoing projects to expand the use of renewable energy in the national grid.

THE ALTAI MOUNTAINS SUBJECT TO CLIMATE CHANGE

Mongolia's unique wildlife and natural beauty have also become a focal point of conservation efforts. The country is home to rare and endangered species, including the snow leopard and the

Bactrian camel, and there are ongoing initiatives to protect these species and their habitats. Ecotourism has emerged as a way to raise awareness of Mongolia's natural heritage while generating income for local communities.

SUMMARY:

The previous chapter explored Mongolia's modern era, a time of significant growth and rapid change. Today, the country balances the pressures of globalisation and environmental challenges with its own deep-rooted cultural heritage. Urbanisation and economic growth are redefining Mongolia's way of life, particularly in its bustling capital, Ulaanbaatar. Mongolia's engagement with international markets, combined with its rich traditions, presents both opportunities and challenges as the nation continues to evolve in an interconnected world.

DID YOU KNOW?

Mongolia's Tsaatan people in the northern Taiga region maintain traditional reindeer herding and produce reindeer milk, a unique but rare commodity. In recent years, reindeer milk has attracted international interest for its distinct flavour and nutritional properties, highlighting the global curiosity surrounding Mongolia's indigenous practices.

PEOPLE

Ukhnaagiin Khürelsükh **(b. 1968)** - Khürelsükh, the current president of Mongolia, has been in office since 2021. He previously served as prime minister from 2017 to 2021 and played a key role in navigating Mongolia through the COVID-19 pandemic. As a member of the Mongolian People's Party (MPP), he has focused on economic recovery, social welfare, and environmental issues, while balancing relations with both China and Russia.

Luvsannamsrain Oyun-Erdene (b. 1980) - Oyun-Erdene is the prime minister of Mongolia, assuming office in 2021. He represents a new generation of leadership and is known for his progressive policies. His government has prioritised economic diversification, technological development, and anti-corruption reforms. Oyun-Erdene has also been instrumental in Mongolia's efforts to reduce its dependence on mining and promote green energy initiatives.

Gombojav Zandanshatar (b. 1970) - As the chairman of the State Great Khural (Mongolia's parliament), Zandanshatar is a key figure in Mongolia's legislative process. He has been a prominent advocate for political and legal reforms, including efforts to strengthen democracy, transparency, and good governance in Mongolia.

PLACES

Ulaanbaatar (Capital and Economic Hub) - Mongolia's capital city remains the political, economic, and cultural heart of the country. With nearly half of Mongolia's population residing in Ulaanbaatar, it faces challenges related to overpopulation, air pollution, and housing. Despite these issues, the city is undergoing rapid modernisation, with new infrastructure, green initiatives, and tech-driven economic projects.

Oyu Tolgoi Mine (Economic Pillar) - Oyu Tolgoi, one of the world's largest copper and gold mines, continues to be a critical driver of Mongolia's economy. The project has drawn substantial foreign investment, particularly from Rio Tinto, and has been central to Mongolia's GDP growth. However, disputes over profit-sharing and environmental concerns remain ongoing.

Khuvsgul Lake (Tourism and Environmental Protection) - Located in northern Mongolia, Khuvsgul Lake is one of the country's most important natural landmarks. It has become a focal point for tourism and environmental conservation. As Mongolia seeks to diversify its economy, sustainable tourism in areas like Khuvsgul is increasingly important, drawing both domestic and international visitors.

EVENTS

Economic Recovery and Diversification (2020s – Present) - Mongolia's economy is heavily reliant on mining, particularly for coal and copper. However, the government under Prime Minister Oyun-Erdene has been making efforts to diversify the economy by promoting renewable energy, technology, and tourism. This diversification strategy is seen as crucial for Mongolia's long-term economic stability and growth, particularly in the face of fluctuating commodity prices.

COVID-19 Pandemic and Vaccination Campaign (2020s) - Mongolia was one of the countries that implemented strict lockdown measures during the COVID-19 pandemic. The government launched an aggressive vaccination campaign, securing vaccines from multiple sources, including China and Russia. The economic impact of the pandemic was significant, leading to downturns in mining and trade, but the country has since been focused on recovery and economic revitalisation.

Anti-Corruption Reforms and Political Stability (2020s – Present) - Corruption has been a longstanding issue in Mongolia, and recent governments have taken steps to address it. Both President Khürelsükh and Prime Minister Oyun-Erdene have pushed for anti-corruption measures, including legal reforms and transparency initiatives. Efforts to root out corruption have been widely supported by the public, although challenges remain in fully implementing these reforms.

Environmental Concerns and Green Energy Initiatives (2020s – Present) - Mongolia's harsh winters and reliance on coal have led to significant air pollution, especially in Ulaanbaatar. In response, the government has been promoting green energy solutions, including solar and wind energy projects. Mongolia's vast, open land makes it an ideal location for renewable energy generation, and the government hopes to position the country as a leader in green energy in the region.

Third Neighbour Policy (Ongoing) - Mongolia continues to navigate its foreign policy through its "Third Neighbour" strategy, balancing its relationships with its two powerful neighbours, Russia and China, while expanding diplomatic, trade, and security ties with other nations like the United States, Japan, and South Korea. This policy aims to ensure Mongolia's sovereignty and economic independence while fostering diverse international partnerships.

Digital Transformation and Innovation (2020s – Present) - The government has made digitalisation a priority, particularly in the wake of the COVID-19 pandemic, which accelerated the need for online services and remote governance. Efforts are underway to modernise the public sector, promote e-governance, and foster a startup ecosystem. The push for innovation also extends to education, with new initiatives aimed at preparing Mongolia's youth for a digital future.

Parliamentary and Presidential Elections (2020 and 2021) - The 2020 parliamentary elections saw the Mongolian People's Party (MPP) maintain control, and in 2021, Ukhnaagiin Khürelsükh was elected president. These elections demonstrated Mongolia's continued commitment to its democratic processes. However, concerns about political dominance by a single party have prompted discussions about maintaining checks and balances within the political system.

Mongolia's Role in Regional Stability (Ongoing) - Mongolia continues to play a role in regional diplomacy, acting as a mediator in East Asian affairs. Its geographic location and political neutrality allow it to facilitate dialogue between nations such as North Korea and South Korea. Mongolia's participation in regional security and diplomatic initiatives reflects its commitment to being a stabilising force in the region.

Climate Change and Desertification (Ongoing) - Mongolia is particularly vulnerable to climate change, with desertification and extreme weather conditions threatening its traditional nomadic lifestyle. The government has initiated environmental projects to combat desertification, such as tree planting and land rehabilitation. However, the challenges posed by climate change remain one of the most significant long-term threats to Mongolia's environment and economy.

CHAPTER 12

The Future of Mongolia

2024 ONWARDS

MONGOLIA'S FUTURE

As Mongolia moves further into the 21st century, it stands poised at the crossroads of opportunity and challenge. Its strategic position between two global powers—Russia and China—presents both diplomatic complexities and economic potential. In recent years, Mongolia has sought to strengthen its role on the global stage, forging new partnerships and navigating the challenges of a rapidly changing world. The country faces a delicate balancing act as it grapples with economic inequality, urbanisation, and the urgent need for environmental sustainability, while continuing to honour the deep-rooted traditions of its nomadic past. The future of Mongolia is one of opportunity, where its unique cultural identity and resilient spirit will play a crucial role in shaping its path forward.

MONGOLIA'S GEOPOLITICAL ROLE (2020S AND BEYOND)

Mongolia's geopolitical significance cannot be overstated, given its location between the two Eurasian giants—Russia and China. Throughout its history, Mongolia has often been influenced by the politics and economics of these two powerful neighbours. In the 21st century, this position continues to shape Mongolia's foreign policy, as it seeks to balance relations with Russia, China, and the broader international community.

China is Mongolia's largest trading partner, with the two countries sharing a long border and deep economic ties, particularly in the mining and energy sectors. Mongolia exports large quantities of coal, copper, and other minerals to China, making this relationship vital to its economic stability. However, this dependence on China has raised concerns about over-reliance on a single partner, leading Mongolian policymakers to seek diversification in both trade and diplomacy.

Russia, Mongolia's historical ally, also plays a critical role in its geopolitical strategy. While economic ties with Russia are not as dominant as with China, the two countries share deep cultural and historical connections, and Russia remains an important partner in energy, defence, and infrastructure projects. Mongolia has maintained a strong relationship with Russia, benefiting from cooperation on key initiatives such as railways and energy supplies, particularly in the form of oil and natural gas.

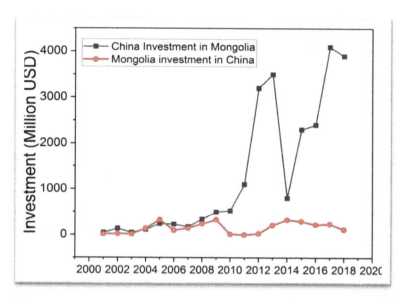

INCREASING INVESTMENT FROM CHINA RISING FEAR OF OVER RELIANCE

In recent years, Mongolia has sought to expand its global engagement through what it calls its "third neighbour" policy, aimed at building closer ties with nations beyond Russia and China. This includes partnerships with countries like the United States, Japan, South Korea, and members of the European Union. Mongolia has positioned itself as a democratic state in a region dominated by authoritarian regimes, which has helped foster goodwill and diplomatic ties with Western nations. Mongolia's participation in international peacekeeping missions and its role as a mediator in regional dialogues have further solidified its reputation as a responsible global actor.

Looking ahead, Mongolia's strategic location and rich natural resources present opportunities for the country to leverage its geopolitical position. Major infrastructure projects, such as transcontinental railways and pipelines, could position Mongolia as a key transit hub for trade between Europe and Asia. However, navigating the complexities of its relationships with Russia, China, and other global powers will require careful diplomacy and strategic foresight.

CHALLENGES AHEAD

Despite its promising economic growth, Mongolia faces significant challenges, particularly related to inequality, urbanisation, and environmental sustainability. The rapid development of the mining sector has created substantial wealth, but this wealth has not been evenly distributed, leading to growing economic disparities between urban and rural populations.

Economic inequality is one of the most pressing issues in Mongolia's future. The prosperity generated by mining and urbanisation has primarily benefited Ulaanbaatar and other major cities, while many rural areas, particularly those dependent on traditional herding, have struggled to keep pace. The divide between the urban middle class and rural herders has widened, with rural communities facing limited access to education, healthcare, and infrastructure. Addressing these disparities will be crucial to ensuring inclusive growth and preventing social unrest.

Urbanisation is another major challenge. Ulaanbaatar, the capital, has seen explosive growth in recent decades, with nearly half of Mongolia's population now living in or around the city. This rapid urbanisation has strained the city's infrastructure, leading to issues such as housing shortages, pollution, and inadequate public services. The growth of informal 'ger' districts on the outskirts of Ulaanbaatar, where many former herders have settled, has highlighted the difficulties of managing urban growth. Finding sustainable solutions to these issues will be essential for Mongolia's long-term development.

Environmental sustainability is perhaps the most urgent challenge facing Mongolia. The country's fragile ecosystem is increasingly under threat from desertification, overgrazing, and climate change. As the Gobi Desert expands and droughts become more frequent, the traditional nomadic way of life is at risk. Herders, who have long depended on the land for their livelihoods, are finding it more difficult to sustain their animals in the face of changing weather patterns and declining pastureland.

ONE OF MANY SOLAR POWER SITES IN MONGOLIA

Climate change poses a particularly acute threat to Mongolia's environment. Rising temperatures, melting glaciers, and more frequent extreme weather events are having a profound impact on both rural and urban communities. Desertification, in particular, threatens the sustainability of Mongolia's agriculture and livestock sectors, which are critical to the livelihoods of many Mongolians.

In response, Mongolia has taken steps to address these environmental challenges. The government has implemented policies aimed at promoting sustainable land use, reforestation, and water conservation. Mongolia has also committed to international climate agreements and has invested in renewable energy projects, including wind and solar power. However, the scale of the environmental challenges facing Mongolia requires continued investment and international cooperation to ensure the country's natural landscape is preserved for future generations.

THE MONGOLIAN SPIRIT

At the heart of Mongolia's future lies its enduring nomadic heritage—a way of life that has shaped the nation's identity for centuries. While modernisation and urbanisation have transformed Mongolia's landscape, the spirit of the nomadic culture remains deeply embedded in the national consciousness. This connection to the land, to the freedom of the steppe, and to the traditions of herding continues to be a source of pride and resilience for the Mongolian people.

The nomadic lifestyle, characterised by mobility, self-reliance, and a deep respect for nature, has withstood the test of time, survived the rise and fall of empires, Soviet rule, and the pressures of globalisation. Today, while many Mongolians have transitioned to urban life, the values and customs of the nomads remain a vital part of Mongolia's identity. Festivals like Naadam, which celebrates traditional Mongolian sports such as wrestling, archery, and horse racing, are a testament to the country's enduring connection to its past.

The challenge for Mongolia in the coming decades will be to preserve this cultural heritage in the face of rapid modernisation. As young Mongolians move to cities in search of education and employment, there is a growing concern that the nomadic way of life could fade into history. However, there are also efforts underway to ensure that these traditions are passed on to future generations. Educational programmes, cultural initiatives, and government policies aimed at supporting rural communities are helping to maintain the connection between Mongolia's past and its future.

In the international arena, Mongolia's nomadic heritage has become a point of distinction, helping the country carve out a unique identity in a globalised world. As Mongolia continues to develop, its ability to balance the demands of modernisation with the preservation of its cultural heritage will be critical to its future success.

UKHNAAGIIN KHÜRELSÜKH MONGOLIA'S CURRENT PRESIDENT IN 2024

SUMMARY:

The journey so far has brought us to the present day, and this final chapter contemplates Mongolia's future. As it moves forward, Mongolia faces pivotal decisions about sustainable development, cultural preservation, and strategic alliances. The challenges of growth, environmental protection, and a complex geopolitical landscape will shape Mongolia's path. In these choices lie the hopes for a future that honours Mongolia's heritage while embracing the possibilities of a new era, ensuring that Mongolia remains resilient, independent, and uniquely Mongolian in a rapidly changing world.

DID YOU KNOW?

Mongolia's aspirations for the future include exploring cutting-edge scientific fields such as asteroid mining. Partnering with international technology firms, Mongolia is investigating the potential of space resource extraction, an ambitious step that illustrates the nation's evolving role in 21st-century global innovation.

PEOPLE

Ukhnaagiin Khürelsükh (b. 1968) - As the current president, Khürelsükh is expected to continue leading Mongolia through its next phase of development. His focus on social welfare, environmental sustainability, and balanced foreign policy will play a significant role in shaping the country's future. He is also expected to further Mongolia's efforts in international diplomacy, particularly in balancing relations with Russia and China while expanding ties with "third neighbours."

Luvsannamsrain Oyun-Erdene (b. 1980) - The sitting prime minister, Oyun-Erdene, is a key figure as Mongolia pushes for economic diversification and technological development. His government's focus on reducing dependency on mining, expanding green energy initiatives, and modernising the public sector will be central to Mongolia's future growth. His leadership will also be crucial in advancing Mongolia's digital transformation and addressing corruption.

New Generation Leaders (Emerging) - As Mongolia enters a new era, younger leaders with a progressive outlook are expected to rise within both government and civil society. These individuals will likely play a key role in modernising Mongolia, particularly in sectors like technology, entrepreneurship, and environmental conservation, as they push for reforms that reflect the needs of the 21st century.

PLACES

Zuunmod (Potential New Development Hub) - As Ulaanbaatar continues to grapple with overpopulation and pollution, Zuunmod, a small city near the capital, is being considered for future development. There are plans to decentralise economic activities and relocate some government offices to alleviate the pressure on Ulaanbaatar, potentially transforming Zuunmod into a secondary hub for political and economic activities.

The Steppe (Nomadic Lifestyle and Climate Impact) - Mongolia's vast steppes will continue to be both an economic and cultural landmark, particularly as climate change increasingly affects nomadic herders. The steppe's future depends on efforts to mitigate desertification, combat overgrazing, and develop sustainable agricultural practices, all of which will shape Mongolia's environmental policies.

Tavantolgoi Power Plant (Future of Energy) - As Mongolia continues to diversify its energy resources, the Tavantolgoi power plant project is crucial. With the aim to meet domestic energy needs and reduce dependence on energy imports, the completion of this project will be a major step in securing Mongolia's energy independence and supporting industrial growth.

EVENTS

Economic Diversification and Technological Innovation (2020s – 2030s) - One of Mongolia's major priorities for the future is reducing its economic reliance on mining, particularly coal and copper exports. The government aims to foster new industries, such as renewable energy, technology, and digital services. Innovations in these sectors will be key to driving future economic growth, while also addressing global demands for sustainability.

Green Energy Transition (2020s – 2040s) - Mongolia has vast potential for solar and wind energy, and there is a growing push to transition away from coal dependency towards renewable energy sources. This shift is crucial not only for economic reasons but also to combat the country's severe air pollution problems and contribute to global efforts in addressing climate change.

Addressing Climate Change and Desertification (Ongoing) - With climate change accelerating, Mongolia faces increased desertification, extreme weather, and a rise in environmental migration. Future policies will focus on combating these effects through land rehabilitation, sustainable grazing practices, and green development projects. How Mongolia navigates these environmental challenges will be crucial for the survival of its traditional nomadic lifestyle.

Balancing Foreign Relations with China, Russia, and the West (Ongoing) - Mongolia's "Third Neighbour" policy will remain to its diplomatic efforts, especially given its strategic location between China and Russia. Strengthening ties with Western countries, while maintaining stable relations with neighbours, will be a significant challenge. Mongolia's ability to navigate complex diplomatic terrains will influence its future political stability and economic opportunities.

Digitalisation and E-Governance (2020s – 2030s) - The government's push for digital transformation will continue to be a critical factor in improving governance, transparency, and public services. E-governance initiatives are expected to modernise the public sector and make Mongolia a more attractive environment for technology and innovation-driven businesses. This will also help to combat corruption by increasing transparency in government operations.

Population Growth and Urbanisation (2020s – 2040s) - Mongolia's population is due to grow over time, with more people migrating to Ulaanbaatar and other urban centres. The challenges of overpopulation, housing shortages, pollution, and infrastructure strain, will be critical for the country's future urban planning efforts. Plans for satellite cities and regional development will be important to decentralising the economy and alleviating the burden on Ulaanbaatar.

Economic Integration in Asia (Ongoing) - As Mongolia seeks to expand its trade relations, particularly with China and Russia, it will likely pursue deeper integration with Asian economic frameworks, such as the Belt and Road Initiative. This presents both opportunities and risks, as Mongolia navigates its geopolitical position between two major powers while ensuring its economic sovereignty.

Education Reform and Workforce Development (2020s – 2040s) - Preparing the next generation for a digital and globalised world will be a critical priority for Mongolia. Education reforms focusing on technology, language skills, and critical thinking will be vital to developing a workforce that can compete in the international market. Investment in higher education and vocational training will be essential for addressing employment challenges and building human capital.

Youth and Civil Society Engagement (Ongoing) - Mongolia's youth are increasingly active in shaping the country's political and social landscape. Civil society organisations focused on environmental conservation, anti-corruption, and human rights are gaining prominence. As the younger generation takes on more leadership roles, their voices will be pivotal in shaping Mongolia's future policies, particularly regarding democracy, transparency, and sustainability.

Mongolia's Role in Global Affairs (2020s – 2040s) - Mongolia will continue to expand its participation in international organisations and forums, contributing to global discussions on climate change, regional security, and human rights. As a democratic nation in a complex geopolitical region, Mongolia's future role as a mediator and advocate for peace and cooperation will grow, particularly in the context of its relationships with North and South Korea and other East Asian nations.

These dates capture important moments in Mongolia's history, illustrating its transformation from a nomadic empire to a modern democratic state with a rich and complex heritage.

209 BCE – Modu Chanyu Unites Xiongnu
Modu Chanyu consolidates power among the nomadic tribes of the Mongolian Steppe, forming the Xiongnu Confederation. This early nomadic empire becomes a significant force in Inner Asia, challenging neighbouring sedentary states.

1206 – Genghis Khan Declares the Mongol Empire
Temüjin, who later takes the title Genghis Khan, unites the Mongol tribes under his rule, establishing the Mongol Empire. This unification marks the beginning of a new era of Mongol dominance and expansion across Asia.

1215 – Mongols Capture Zhongdu (Beijing)
Genghis Khan's forces capture Zhongdu, the capital of the Jin Dynasty in northern China. This victory demonstrates the Mongols' military prowess and marks a pivotal moment in their conquest of China.

1227 – Death of Genghis Khan
Genghis Khan dies during a campaign in Western Xia. His death marks the end of an era but also the continuation of his legacy through his successors, who further expand the empire.

1236–1242 – Mongol Invasions of Europe
Led by Batu Khan, the Mongols embark on a series of invasions into Eastern Europe, affecting regions such as Russia, Hungary, and Poland. These invasions have a significant impact on European history and the geopolitical landscape of the region.

1271 – Establishment of the Yuan Dynasty
Kublai Khan, a grandson of Genghis Khan, formally establishes the Yuan Dynasty in China. This marks the beginning of Mongol rule over China and the transformation of the Mongol Empire into a significant global power.

1368 – Fall of the Yuan Dynasty
The Yuan Dynasty is overthrown by the Ming Dynasty, leading to the retreat of the Mongols from China. This marks the end of Mongol political dominance in China but does not diminish their influence in the wider region.

1691 – Mongolia Becomes a Protectorate of the Qing Dynasty
Following years of internal conflict and external pressures, the Khalkha Mongols submit to the Manchu Qing Dynasty, leading to Mongolia's incorporation into the Qing Empire as a protectorate.

1911 – Mongolia Declares Independence from Qing China
In the wake of the Qing Dynasty's collapse, Mongolia, under the leadership of Bogd Khan, declares its independence. This move is driven by nationalist sentiments and aspirations for sovereignty.

1921 – Mongolian Revolution and Soviet Support
The Mongolian Revolution, supported by Soviet forces, overthrows the Bogd Khan government. This revolution leads to the establishment of a socialist government and marks Mongolia's alignment with Soviet communism.

1924 – Formation of the Mongolian People's Republic
Following the death of Bogd Khan, Mongolia officially becomes the Mongolian People's Republic. This new communist state is heavily influenced by Soviet policies and marks a significant shift in Mongolia's political structure.

1937–1939 – Stalinist Purges in Mongolia
Under Stalinist influence, Mongolia experiences a series of political purges. Thousands, including intellectuals, political opponents, and

Buddhist clergy, are executed or imprisoned, reflecting the harshness of Soviet-style governance.

1990 – Democratic Revolution
A wave of peaceful protests leads to the collapse of the communist regime. This pivotal moment ushers in a new era of democracy, with multi-party elections and increased political freedoms.

1992 – New Democratic Constitution
Mongolia adopts a new constitution that establishes it as a democratic republic. The constitution enshrines principles of democracy, human rights, and the rule of law, marking a significant milestone in Mongolia's transition to democracy.

2004 – Mongolia Joins the United Nations Peacekeeping Forces
Mongolia begins participating in international peacekeeping missions under the United Nations. This marks a commitment to global peace and security and highlights Mongolia's active role in international affairs.

2011 – 100th Anniversary of Independence
Mongolia celebrates the centenary of its declaration of independence from Qing China. This milestone reaffirms the country's national sovereignty and is commemorated with significant national pride and reflection.

These key leaders reflect Mongolia's rich and evolving history, from its imperial past to its modern political landscape.

Genghis Khan (c. 1162–1227) - Genghis Khan, born Temüjin, unified the Mongol tribes and established the Mongol Empire. His innovative military strategies and conquests laid the foundation for one of the largest empires in history, impacting global events across Eurasia.

Kublai Khan (1215–1294) - Grandson of Genghis Khan, Kublai Khan founded the Yuan Dynasty in China. His reign saw the integration of Mongol and Chinese cultures, promotion of trade along the Silk Road, and expansion of Mongol influence into Southeast Asia.

Ögedei Khan (1186–1241) - The third Great Khan of the Mongol Empire, continued his father's conquests with campaigns into Eastern Europe and the Middle East. His administration established a more structured empire and centralised authority.

Möngke Khan (1209–1259) - The fourth Great Khan, Möngke Khan's reign focused on consolidating Mongol rule and expanding into the Middle East and Central Asia. His efforts included administrative reforms but were cut short by his death during a campaign.

Bogd Khan (1869–1924) - Mongolia's last king before the communist era. He led Mongolia's struggle for independence following the collapse of the Qing Dynasty, though his rule faced significant internal and external challenges.

Jebe (d. 1225) - A trusted general of Genghis Khan, Jebe played a key role in the Mongol conquests of Khwarezm and Central Asia, demonstrating remarkable military skill and strategic acumen.

Subutai (c. 1176–1248) - A leading Mongol general and strategist under Genghis Khan and Ögedei Khan, was instrumental in the successful military campaigns across Eastern Europe and the Middle East.

Yelu Chucai (1190–1244) - A Chinese scholar and advisor to Genghis Khan, known for his contributions to the Mongol Empire's administration and economy, particularly in tax and financial reforms.

Abaqa Khan (1234–1282) - The third ruler of the Ilkhanate, Abaqa Khan expanded its territory and established stability in Persia and Central Asia through military campaigns and effective governance.

Tamerlane (Timur) (c. 1336–1405) - Founded the Timurid Empire and expanded it across Central Asia, Persia, and the Middle East. His empire was influenced by Mongol military strategies and traditions.

Altan Khan (1507–1582) - A leader of the Tümed Mongols, resisted Ming Dynasty encroachment and worked to consolidate Mongol power in northern China during the late 16th century.

Jebtsundamba Khutuktu (1870–1924) - Also known as Bogd Khan, served as Mongolia's spiritual leader and king, leading the country's early 20th-century independence efforts until the establishment of the communist government.

Khorloogiin Choibalsan (1895–1952) - A key figure in Mongolia's communist era, aligning the country with the Soviet Union and implementing communist policies during his leadership.

Jambyn Batmönkh (1939–1993) - President of Mongolia from 1984 to 1990, playing a role in the transition towards democracy and the end of communist rule.

Punsalmaagiin Ochirbat (b. 1938) - First democratically elected President of Mongolia, served from 1990 to 1996, overseeing the country's shift from communist rule to a democratic government.

Nambaryn Enkhbayar (b. 1958) - President of Mongolia from 2005 to 2009, addressing economic and social issues and contributing to the country's political development during the early 21st century.

Khaltmaagiin Battulga (b. 1963) - Served in Battulga served as President from 2017 to 2021, focusing on international relations and domestic challenges such as corruption and economic development.

Ukhnaagiin Khürelsükh (b. 1968) - Prime Minister from 2016 to 2020 and President from 2021 onwards, has emphasised economic reforms, anti-corruption measures, and enhancing Mongolia's global standing.

NOTABLE MONGOLIANS IN THE ARTS AND LITERACY

Mongolia's artistic and literary heritage shines through. From literature to music and theatre, these artists have shaped Mongolia's cultural identity, blending tradition with modernity.

Dulduityn Danzanravjaa (1803–1856) - Known as the "Terrible Saint", Danzanravjaa was a famous poet, playwright, and lama. He made significant contributions to Mongolian Buddhist literature and culture, founded schools and theatres, and was known for his progressive views on education and gender equality.

Byambyn Rinchen (1905–1977) - A highly influential writer, linguist, and translator. He contributed greatly to Mongolian literature and is known for translating classical works from Russian, German, and French. His work was instrumental in the revival of Mongolian national identity through literature.

Dashdorjiin Natsagdorj (1906–1937) - Considered the founder of modern Mongolian literature, Natsagdorj's works, including the famous poem "My Homeland" (Minii nutag), are iconic. Despite his short life, his influence on Mongolian literature has been profound.

Tsendiin Damdinsüren (1908–1986) - Damdinsüren was a leading Mongolian poet and writer, pivotal in shaping modern Mongolian literature. He is best known for writing the lyrics of Mongolia's national anthem and for his poetry and prose that reflect Mongolian traditions and social changes.

Gonchigiin Birvaa (1922–2006) - Birvaa was a prominent Mongolian composer, creating some of Mongolia's most well-known operatic works. His compositions, combining traditional Mongolian folk music with modern influences, remain widely performed.

126

Natsagdorjiin Tsultem (1923–2001) - Tsultem was a celebrated painter and art historian. His paintings often depicted Mongolian history and nomadic life. He played a key role in developing modern Mongolian art and conducted research into ancient Mongolian artistic traditions.

Lodongiin Tudev (b. 1935) - A highly respected writer, editor, and politician. He has authored numerous novels, short stories, and essays, and was actively involved in shaping Mongolia's cultural policy during the socialist period.

Gonchigiin Jargal (b. 1947) - A distinguished sculptor known for his large-scale sculptures that often reflect traditional Mongolian themes. His work has been exhibited internationally and is renowned for blending contemporary and traditional elements.

Gonchigiin Sukhbaatar (b. 1947) - A leading theatre director known for his innovative productions of both classical and contemporary plays. He has been a key figure in modernising Mongolian theatre while retaining traditional storytelling methods.

Chinghiziin Khulan (b. 1979) - A contemporary Mongolian poet, Khulan has gained international recognition for her evocative and lyrical poetry. Her works, translated into multiple languages, explore themes of identity, nature, and Mongolia's nomadic spirit.

NOTABLE MONGOLIAN INVENTIONERS, SCIENTISTS AND TECHNOLOGISTS

Mongolia's scientific and technological progress has been driven by pioneers in engineering, geology, agriculture, and environmental science. These innovators across diverse fields have shaped Mongolia's modern scientific landscape.

Jambyn Lkhümbe (1906–1934) - An engineer and one of the first Mongolian experts in mechanical engineering. He was instrumental in introducing modern engineering techniques to Mongolia, contributing to the early industrialisation of the country during the socialist period.

Byambyn Dash-Yondon (1919–1992) - A prominent geologist and academic. He contributed significantly to geological studies in Mongolia, particularly in the areas of mineral resources and tectonics. He also played a crucial role in the development of Mongolia's mining industry and was a respected figure in the scientific community.

Sonomyn Luvsangombo (1922–1993) - A pioneering agricultural scientist. His research in crop science and sustainable agricultural practices played a critical role in improving food security in Mongolia. He introduced modern farming techniques that helped increase agricultural productivity in the country's harsh climate.

Shagdaryn Bira (b. 1927) - A historian and scholar with a strong background in the history of science and technology in Mongolia. His research has documented the technological innovations of ancient and medieval Mongolia, particularly during the Mongol Empire, highlighting the region's contributions to global science.

Namjilyn Norovbanzad (1931–2002) - A scientist and academic who specialised in veterinary medicine. Her work on animal diseases, particularly in the study of infectious diseases in livestock, greatly advanced veterinary science in Mongolia.

Tseveenravdangiin Nyamdavaa (b. 1948) - A prominent scientist in the field of environmental science and ecology. His research focuses on the impact of climate change on Mongolia's ecosystems. He has contributed to policies aimed at preserving Mongolia's unique landscapes and biodiversity while promoting sustainable development.

Damdinjavyn Baatar (b. 1950) – A scientist specialising in chemistry and materials science. His work in developing advanced materials for industrial and environmental applications has earned him recognition both in Mongolia and internationally. He has made contributions to areas such as nanotechnology and sustainable materials.

Yondongiin Otgonbayar (b. 1957) - A respected physicist who has made significant contributions to nuclear physics and plasma research. His work has helped place Mongolia on the global map in the field of scientific research, particularly through his involvement in international collaborations on nuclear fusion.

Dashdorjyn Ganbold (b. 1961) - A computer scientist and one of the leading figures in the development of Mongolia's information technology sector. He played a key role in establishing Mongolia's internet infrastructure and has worked to advance digital technologies in both public and private sectors.

Tseren-Ochiryn Davaadorj (b. 1965) - An engineer and inventor, known for his work in renewable energy. He has designed several innovative systems for harnessing wind and solar energy, which have been utilised in rural Mongolia to provide sustainable energy solutions in off-grid areas.

Mongolia is shaped by its nomadic history, Buddhist beliefs, and the legacy of the Mongol Empire. The cultural practices, festivals, and daily life of Mongolians reflect centuries-old customs that have been passed down through generations.

Nomadic Lifestyle - At the heart of Mongolia's cultural identity is its nomadic heritage, which has shaped the way of life for many Mongolians for centuries. The nomadic lifestyle revolves around the herding of livestock, including horses, yaks, camels, sheep, and goats, and a deep connection to the land and nature. Mongolian nomads live in portable, round felt tents called gers (also known as yurts), which are designed to withstand the harsh climate of the Mongolian Steppe. This semi-nomadic lifestyle requires families to move with the seasons in search of better pastures for their animals, fostering a strong sense of self-reliance and adaptation.

The importance of the horse in Mongolian culture cannot be overstated. Horses are integral to everyday life, transportation, and even spiritual practices. Mongolians are renowned for their horsemanship, with children learning to ride from a very young age. Horses are also central to many traditional sports and festivals, reflecting the deep bond between Mongolians and these animals.

The Legacy of Genghis Khan - The legacy of Genghis Khan, the founder of the Mongol Empire in the 13th century, remains an integral part of Mongolia's national identity. Genghis Khan united the Mongol tribes and created one of the largest empires in history, stretching from East Asia to Europe. His legacy is celebrated not only for his military achievements but also for his contributions to trade, law, and cultural exchange along the Silk Road.

Many Mongolians take great pride in their connection to Genghis Khan, and his image and name are still widely used in national symbols, monuments, and even popular culture. The reverence for this historical figure continues to play a key role in shaping Mongolian patriotism and cultural identity.

Mongolian Buddhism - Buddhism, specifically Tibetan Buddhism, is the dominant religion in Mongolia and plays a significant role in the country's cultural and spiritual traditions. Buddhism was first introduced to Mongolia in the 16th century, and over the centuries, it became deeply rooted in the daily lives of the Mongolian people. Monasteries and temples are scattered across the country, serving as centres of religious life and cultural preservation. Many Mongolians visit these sacred sites to pray, offer donations, and participate in religious ceremonies.

Despite periods of suppression during the Soviet era, when many monasteries were destroyed, Mongolian Buddhism has seen a resurgence since the 1990s, with a revival of traditional practices and the restoration of important religious sites. Gandantegchinlen Monastery in Ulaanbaatar is one of the most important and active monasteries, serving as a hub for Buddhist learning and rituals.

Shamanism and Nature Worship - Alongside Buddhism, shamanism remains a vital spiritual tradition in Mongolia. Shamanism is the oldest belief system in the country and is deeply connected to nature. It involves the worship of ancestral spirits, as well as natural elements such as the sky, earth, water, and fire. Tengriism, the ancient Mongolian belief in the Sky God Tengri, is central to shamanistic practices, reflecting a reverence for the natural world and the elements.

Shamans, believed to have the ability to communicate with spirits and heal the sick, still play important roles in some rural communities. Mongolians often observe rituals to honour spirits and seek protection or blessings for their herds and families, particularly during significant life events such as births, weddings, and funerals.

Naadam Festival - One of the most important cultural events in Mongolia is the annual Naadam Festival, celebrated in July. Often referred to as the "Three Manly Games," Naadam features three traditional Mongolian sports - wrestling, horse racing, and archery. These events date back to the time of Genghis Khan and remain a vital expression of Mongolian identity.

- *Mongolian wrestling (known as Bökh)* is the most popular sport in the country, and Naadam wrestling matches draw huge crowds. Competitors wear traditional wrestling attire and follow ancient customs, such as performing a symbolic eagle dance before and after each match.
- *Horse racing* at Naadam is unique, with races covering long distances (up to 30 km), and the riders are often young children. The endurance of both horses and riders is celebrated, reflecting the deep cultural importance of horses.
- *Archery competitions*, using traditional Mongolian bows and arrows, are held during Naadam as well. Both men and women participate in archery, showcasing their precision and skill.

Naadam is not only a sports festival but also a celebration of Mongolian heritage, with traditional music, dance, and colourful costumes enriching the atmosphere.

Traditional Clothing - Deel, the traditional Mongolian garment, is worn by both men and women and has remained largely unchanged for centuries. The deel is a long, loose robe tied at the waist with a sash and often made from bright, colourful fabrics. The design of the deel varies slightly between regions and is typically worn during special occasions, festivals, and everyday life in rural areas.

The Mongolian hat, or loovuuz, is another important cultural symbol, particularly worn during ceremonies and by elders. Different styles of hats indicate social status and regional origins.

Traditional Music and Dance - Mongolia has a rich musical heritage, with traditional throat singing (known as khoomei) being one of the most distinctive forms. Khoomei is a unique style of overtone singing where the performer produces two or more pitches simultaneously. This form of music is believed to have originated among nomadic herders and is closely associated with nature and the sound of wind, rivers, and animals.

Morin Khuur, or the horsehead fiddle, is the national musical instrument of Mongolia. The instrument's design, featuring a carved horse's head, and its sound evoke the importance of horses in Mongolian life. It is often played during ceremonial occasions and is a key part of Mongolian folk music.

Traditional Mongolian dance, such as the Biyelgee, often features movements that mimic everyday activities of nomadic life, such as horse riding and milking animals. These dances are performed at celebrations and festivals and are accompanied by traditional music.

Cuisine and Hospitality - Mongolian cuisine is heavily influenced by the country's nomadic lifestyle, with a focus on meat and dairy products. Mutton, yak, and goat are staple meats, often cooked in simple ways such as boiling or grilling. Buuz (steamed dumplings filled with meat) and khuushuur (fried meat pies) are popular traditional dishes. Airag, a fermented mare's milk, is a traditional drink enjoyed during festivals and special occasions.

Hospitality is a core value in Mongolian culture, and guests are treated with great respect and generosity. Visitors to a Mongolian ger are often offered food and drink as a sign of hospitality, with milk tea and dairy products frequently served.

Mongolia has produced many exceptional athletes who have made significant contributions to both national and international sports.

Jambyn Batmönkh (1936–1997) – A distinguished chess player who became an International Master in 1968. Although he is more widely recognised for his political role as Chairman of the Presidium of the People's Great Khural, his accomplishments in chess were remarkable and made him one of the most respected figures in Mongolian sports and political history.

Khorloogiin Bayanmönkh (b. 1944) - A legendary Mongolian wrestler who made a name for himself internationally. He won a silver medal in freestyle wrestling at the 1972 Munich Olympics and became a world wrestling champion in 1974. Bayanmönkh's dominance in wrestling, both domestically and internationally, has earned him widespread recognition as one of Mongolia's greatest athletes.

Badmaanyambuugiin Bat-Erdene (b. 1964) - One of Mongolia's most decorated traditional wrestlers. He won the Naadam Championship an extraordinary 11 times, a record few have come close to matching. Beyond his success in wrestling, Bat-Erdene has served as a member of the Mongolian Parliament, demonstrating his influence in both sport and politics.

Dolgorsürengiin Dagvadorj (b. 1980) - Known by his sumo name Asashōryū Akinori, Dagvadorj was the first Mongolian-born wrestler to achieve the prestigious rank of yokozuna, the highest rank in sumo wrestling. Over the course of his career, he won 25 top division championships, making him one of the most successful and well-known sumo wrestlers of all time.

Naidangiin Tüvshinbayar (b. 1984) - Mongolia's first Olympic gold medallist, having won the top prize in the men's 100kg judo category at the 2008 Beijing Olympics. His victory was a historic moment for the nation, and he followed it up with a silver medal at the 2012 London Olympics, solidifying his status as a national icon in judo.

Mönkhbatyn Davaajargal (b. 1984) - More famously known as Hakuho Shō, Mönkhbatyn Davaajargal is a Mongolian-born sumo wrestler who has set unprecedented records in Japan. With 45 tournament championships, he is the most successful sumo wrestler in history. Hakuho's dominance in the sport from the mid-2000s until his retirement in 2021 makes him one of the greatest sumo wrestlers of all time.

Baatarjavyn Shoovdor (b. 1990) - A top-tier freestyle wrestler who has won multiple international medals, including a bronze medal at the 2018 World Wrestling Championships. She has represented Mongolia at various global competitions and continues to be one of the nation's most successful female wrestlers.

Sumiya Dorjsuren (b. 1991) – A judoka who became a national hero after winning a silver medal at the 2016 Rio Olympics in the women's lightweight division. In 2017, she achieved even greater success by becoming the World Judo Champion, further elevating her status as one of the top judokas in Mongolia.

INDEX

These resources offer valuable information and insights into various aspects of Mongolian history and culture, making them useful for anyone looking to explore the subject further.

BOOKS

"Genghis Khan and the Making of the Modern World" by Jack Weatherford provides a detailed account of Genghis Khan's impact on global history and the establishment of the Mongol Empire.

"The Secret History of the Mongol Queens: The Women Who Ruled the Mongol Empire" by Jack Weatherford explores the roles of Mongol women in the empire, shedding light on their influence and leadership.

"The History of the Mongol Conquests" by J.J. Saunders is an academic work that offers a comprehensive overview of the Mongol conquests and their historical context.

"The Mongol Empire" by John Andrew Boyle is a classic historical account that covers the rise and expansion of the Mongol Empire.

"The Mongols" by David Morgan is an accessible and insightful book on the Mongol Empire's history, culture, and impact on the world.

"Mongolia: The Rise and Fall of the Empire" by Robert Marshall provides a thorough examination of Mongolia's historical rise, its empire, and eventual decline.

"The Cambridge History of Inner Asia: The Chinggisid Age," edited by Nicola Di Cosmo is a scholarly collection of essays on the Chinggisid era, offering a comprehensive view of the Mongol Empire's influence on Inner Asia.

"Mongolia and the Mongol Empire" by Peter Jackson provides an in-depth look at the history and administration of the Mongol Empire.

"The History of Mongolia" by I. A. Zhamtsarano is an authoritative historical text covering Mongolia from its early history to the modern era.

"Mongolian Nomadic Society: A Comparative Analysis" by Uradyn E. Bulag explores Mongolian nomadic culture and society, offering insights into its historical development.

"The Rise and Fall of the Yuan Dynasty" by William E. Welsh is a detailed study of the Yuan Dynasty's impact on Chinese and Mongolian history.

"Mongolian History: A Textbook" by Ts. Munkh-Erdene offers a comprehensive overview of Mongolian history from ancient times to the present.

"Mongolian Politics in the 20th Century" by B. Khishigjargal examines Mongolia's political evolution through the 20th century.

"Mongolia: A Political History" by Thomas J. Barfield analyses Mongolia's political history, with a focus on its transition from communism to democracy.

"The Mongol Empire and Its Legacy," edited by David O. Morgan is a collection of essays on the legacy of the Mongol Empire and its influence on world history.

Metropolitan Museum of Art - Provides articles and images related to Mongolian art and history.
https://www.metmuseum.org/toah/hd/mong/hd_mong.htm

Mongolian National Historical Museum - Offers resources and information about Mongolian history and cultural heritage.
https://mnmuseum.gov.mn/

Mongolia's Digital Archives - Provide digital resources and documents related to Mongolian history.
https://www.archives.mn/

Encyclopaedia Britannica - Includes entries on Mongolian history, including key figures and historical events.
https://www.britannica.com/place/Mongolia

Columbia Electronic Encyclopedia - Features articles on Mongolian history, culture, and key historical figures.
https://www.encyclopedia.com

BULGARIA THROUGH THE AGES

CYPRUS THROUGH THE AGES

UKRAINE THROUGH THE AGES

ROMANIA THROUGH THE AGES

WALES THROUGH THE AGES

ICELAND THROUGH THE AGES

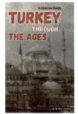

TURKEY THROUGH THE AGES

MALTA THROUGH THE AGES

SCOTLAND THROUGH THE AGES

GREECE THROUGH THE AGES

SERBIA THROUGH THE AGES

FRANCE THROUGH THE AGES

NORTH MACEDONIA THROUGH THE AGES

ENGLAND THROUGH THE AGES

GIBRALTAR THROUGH THE AGE

www.ingramcontent.com/pod-product-compliance
Lightning Source LLC
Chambersburg PA
CBHW050459080326
40788CB00001B/3908